College Cooking

with Julie

- ☑ **Affordable**
- ☑ **Healthy**
- ☑ **Simple**
- ☑ **Quick**

Julie Hoffman

Library of Congress Control Number: 2009906848
ISBN: 978-0-615-29393-6

Manufactured by

Favorite Recipes® Press

an imprint of

FRP®INC

A wholly owned subsidiary of Southwestern/Great American, Inc.
P. O Box 305142
Nashville, Tennessee 37230
1-800-358-0560

1st Printing 2009

www.collegecookingwithjulie.com
collegecookingwithjulie@gmail.com

College Cooking

with *Julie*

By Julie Hoffman

with photographs by David K. Dismukes, CPP

About Julie

I got an early cooking education at home, my grandmother's kitchen and at O'Shea's, the family owned restaurant on Marco Island, Florida. From years of active kitchen participation, I learned how to blend my mom's quick health conscious meals and my grandmother's authentic Italian cooking with food business efficiency. I combined these ingredients with what I considered the best episodes from the Food Network channel into the vast bowl of trial and error experience.

While completing a finance degree at Auburn University, I was surprised how few students really knew much about cooking. My goal in writing this book was to create an exciting guide for students, who need to eat healthy, who are on limited budgets and want to create great tasting food as quickly as possible. The recipes will give you, your roommates and friends value-based, tasty meals that are fun and easy to make. Food and finance go together more than ever!

In Loving Memory of:

Grandma Shea
&
Gram Hoffman

Contents

Introduction..8

Basic Equipment...11

Study Time Snacks..12
- Sweet Potato Fries
- Terrific Trail Mix
- Frozen Banana Popsicles
- Vanilla-Berry Smoothie
- Cottage Cheese, Fruit and Granola
- Jazzed-up Rice Cake
- Chicken Ranch Wrap
- Ground Chicken Meatballs

Decadent Dips...22
- Hummus Dip
- Guacamole Dip
- Spinach Artichoke Dip
- Healthy and Hearty Dip
- Buffalo Chicken Dip
- Mexican Dip
- Cream Cheese and Salsa Dip
- Super Bowl Dip

Crowd Pleasers 32
- Italian Pasta Salad
- Cucumber and Bacon Sandwich
- Marshmallow and Lime Fresh Fruit Salad
- Mexican Salad
- The "Simple Salad"
- Beer Brats and Caramelized Onions
- Orange Cup Sweet Potatoes

Comfort Foods..42
- Viva La Difference Lasagna
- Tuna Melt
- Classy Grilled Cheese
- Peanut Butter and Jelly French Toast
- Creamy Dreamy Mashies
- O'Shea's Famous Clam Chowder
- Fancy Mac and Cheese

Dropping the Freshmen 15...52
- Veggie Soup
- Strawberry-Banana Smoothie
- Pear and Gorgonzola Salad
- Spinach Apple Salad
- Strawberry Feta Salad
- Grilled Turkey Burgers
- Grilled Shrimp and Asparagus
- Spaghetti Squash
- The Any White Fish DIsh
- Healthy Eggy Goodness
- Yogurt Blast

Pinchin' Pennies 64
- New Orleans Rib Sticker
- Tuna Pasta
- BBQ Chicken Legs and Baked Beans
- Ramen Tuna
- Erin's Ramen P-a-a-r-r-t-a-y
- Chicken Spaghetti
- Pasta Meat Salad
- Homemade Chili

Date Night Dinners 74
- Shrimp Scampi
- Ground Turkey Meatloaf
- Rosemary Orange Roasted Chicken
- Red Pepper and Dill Salmon
- BBQ Chicken Pizza
- Pork Chops Smothered in Caramelized Onions
- Veal Scaloppini
- Steak Stir-Fry

Dorm Dishes 84
- Hotdog and Baked Beans
- Quesadilla
- Shrimp and Grits
- White Fish with Cheesy Broccoli and a Baked Potato
- Grilled Chicken Caesar Salad
- Breakfast Burrito
- Spinach and Pancetta with Wild Rice

Veggie Love 92
- Margarita Pizza
- Asparagus and Cherry Tomato Angel Hair
-Roasted Veggie Couscous
- Eggplant Parmesan
- Portobello and Swiss Sandwich

Sinful Sweets 100
- Perfect Strawberry Cake
- Nana Lombardo's Secret Biscotti Recipe
-Lemon-Berry Cupcakes
- Blissful Banana Bread
- Almond Snowball Cookies
- Tropical Rum Cake
-Carefree Carrot Cake
- Gram's Crannberry Muffins
- Fruity-Tootie Crumble

Weekly Planning 112

Special Thanks 116

Introduction

Cooking in college is a win-win situation

- **Save money** (yes, fast-food adds up quickly).

- **Eat healthy** (when you cook, YOU know what goes into the meal).

- **Bring people together** with your impressive cooking skills. (I make the chore of cooking fun!)

- **Time management** (planning meals ahead and allowing for left-overs, leaves more time for the books and bars).

- **Relaxing experience** (chopping, mashing, mixing, stuffing; believe it or not, this can be a stress reliever, especially after hearing Professor Monotone blab for an hour).

I use the "$" symbol to illustrate estimated meal costs as follows::

- **$$$** - High or expensive which is over $20

- **$$** - Medium cost range between $10-$20

- **$** - Most affordable under $10

(note: prices vary depending on geographic location)

Key points of my college cooking philosophy

- Don't stress out by trying to follow recipes exactly. I built simplicity into ingredient choices and cooking procedures. Most mistakes can be remedied and should be considered opportunities for creativity.

- Learn to have fun estimating. Cooking is thinking. I use '"working" measurement descriptions like: handful, dash, scoop and splash often, which means small hand size amounts. You can always add, but it is hard to take away, or neutralize too much.

- When possible plan ahead and have the basic ingredients for most meals always on hand. Never run out of salt/pepper, sugar, olive oil, cheese, fresh bread/tortillas, onions, apples, peanut butter, etc.

- Most of these meals have been deliberately designed to provide leftovers, which for the next three days can be healthy, tasty, and economical.

- Have your prep work (vegetables diced, fruit chopped) done and within hands reach before you begin the art of cooking.

Julie's List of "DUH's"

I don't state the obvious in my directions....so listen up now!

- Wash your fruits and veggies thoroughly before using!

- Don't use a dull knife. That's usually how people end up cutting themselves.

- Be careful when handling any raw meat or chicken! Wash hands thoroughly with soap and water after handling to avoid cross-contamination. Try to use only one hand for touching meat, so you don't end up contaminating everything in the kitchen.

- It is very important to wash hands properly before cooking or eating. Use warm water, soap and rub vigorously for at least 15 to 20 seconds, or as my mom says, sing the ABC song. Scrub all surfaces, including back of hands, wrists and between fingers. Rinse well. Dry hands with a clean or disposable towel. Use the towel to turn off the faucet (You don't want to touch the germy faucet with your clean hands!).

- FYI min = minute.

Down and Dirty Basic Equipment

What to buy before going to college:

Basics:

- Knives: Paring and Chef (small and large knife)
- Pans: 12" skillet and 6" nonstick skillet
- Pots: 2 and 8-quart pot with covers
- Two baking sheets
- 9"x13" baking pan
- Two 9" round cake pans
- Cutting board (plastic for raw meats; wooden for fruits and vegetables)
- Can opener

Utensils:

- Spatula
- Whisk
- Ladle
- Wooden, metal and a slotted spoon (3 separate spoons)
- Tongs

Optional, but highly recommended:

- Glass measuring cup
- Measuring spoons
- Colander (steel or plastic)
- Grater (with various size holes)
- Electric, hand-held mixer
- Blender
- 12-cup muffin tin
- Vegetable peeler
- Mortar or pestle
- Two cooking racks
- Meat thermometer
- Pot holder or oven mitts

Study Time *Snacks*

D o you ever keep track of what you stuff in your mouth as you grow glassy-eyed reading a boring textbook? Come on, if you chew up and down as you read side to side your tummy and thighs will get fat and wide. I know it sounds bad, but you know it's the truth. When I study for long periods of time I typically take breaks in front of an open refrigerator. As I scan this cold food closet, knowing I am not that hungry, my mouth still waters for a smooth slice of chocolate cake. Whether procrastinating, dreaming, or feeling the pull of sweet pleasures – just get a grip and re-focus girlfriend!

What you choose to snack on during crunch-time affects your level of concentration. Any big sugar fix will buzz out your bod in less than a half hour! Where will your brain be then? Welcome to my world of low sugar, high energy and mind mentoring snacks, drinks and short meals.

This chapter gives you many food options based on prep time, study time and everything in between. Just because studying has chained you to your desk or your bed doesn't mean you shouldn't explore healthy food and drink choices.

Sweet Potato Fries

These can be addicting... because they are. Sweet, salty and crispy... enough said.

NEED:
- Few splashes of canola oil
- 1 sweet potato, peeled and cut into thin strips (think French fry)
- Couple pinches of salt

TO DO:
1) Drizzle enough canola oil to lightly cover bottom of pan on medium heat.
2) Add the sweet potato strips and keep flipping around using two forks or tongs.
3) Cook until each side is golden brown.
4) Place on a paper towel to collect excess grease.
5) Sprinkle with salt.

- ✓ Prep-time: 4 min
- ✓ Cook-time: about 8-10 min
- ✓ Cost Factor: $
- ✓ Serves: 1-2

Terrific Trail Mix

I have a zip-lock bag of this in my backpack, purse, AND by my bed at just about all times. This trail mix is an all-star healthy combination giving you energy and crunch, while still satisfying your natural salty and sweet cravings.

NEED:

- Walnuts and/or almonds (you need at least 1 healthy nut!)
- Raisins
- Peanuts (salted or unsalted)
- Banana chips
- Dark chocolate chips or dark chocolate M&M's (go DARK… antioxidants!)
- Granola (store bought — I know, I'm cheating! But, saves you time and $!)

TO DO:

1) Place a handful (large, small, or multiple) of each ingredient in a large mixing bowl and toss around with hands.
2) Put the mix either in one large zip-lock bag, in a few small individual zip-lock bags, or a container — which m,ever is most convenient for you.

- ✓ Prep-time: 2 min
- ✓ Cost Factor: $$$
- ✓ Serves: about 8 (depends)

Frozen Banana Popsicles

This will hit the spot!

NEED:

- 4 large bananas, peeled and cut in half
- 2 cups semisweet chocolate chips
- 2 scoops butter
- 8 popsicle sticks

TO DO:

1) Take popsicle stick and poke flat end through each banana half, leaving out enough stick to use as a handle.
2) Freeze bananas for about an hour.
3) Melt chocolate chips and butter in a small pot on low heat.
4) Coat each banana with chocolate by dipping and using a spoon for extra help.
5) Put bananas back in the freezer on wax paper until frozen and store in an air-tight container.

Tip — Don't want to add chocolate? Just slice bananas, put them in a zip-lock bag, and freeze for a quick, cold, creamy snack.

✓ Prep-time: 7 min
✓ Cook-time: about 8 min
✓ Cost Factor: $
✓ Serves: 8

Vanilla-Berry Smoothie

This is a hydrating, refreshing, and nutritious snack that will keep you going strong without you feeling sluggish or weighed down.

NEED:

- 1 large handful of frozen or fresh mixed berries
- 1 large scoop of vanilla yogurt
- 1 handful of ice
- Splash of skim milk or fruit juice
- 1 dash of vanilla extract (optional)

TO DO:

1) Throw all ingredients in a blender and blend away! Add more of any ingredients to suit your preference.

✓ Prep-time: 3 min
✓ Cost Factor: $
✓ Serves: 1

Cottage Cheese, Fruit and Granola

Healthy, healthy, healthy! No sugar lows here! This is a rewarding and fulfilling snack between the gym and the books. You can use ANY fruit you have on hand. No rules!

NEED:

- 1 large scoop low-fat or skim cottage cheese
- Few grapes, halved
- ½ apple, bite-sized chunks
- 1 small handful cantaloupe, bite-sized chunks
- 1 small handful granola or dry cereal

TO DO:

1) Combine all ingredients in a bowl and grub on!

> ✓ Prep-time: 6 min
> ✓ Cost Factor: $$ (depends-choosing seasonal fruit?)
> ✓ Serves: 1

Jazzed-up Rice Cake

This snack offers crunch, cream, and crisp! This combo will hold you over between meals, while sustaining high-energy levels.

NEED:
- 1 large round rice cake (flavor? Up to you — I prefer caramel)
- 1 small spoonful of peanut butter (TRY not to O.D. on it… I know, it's hard!)
- ½ apple, thinly sliced
- Small handful of raisins

TO DO:
1) Spread a thin layer of peanut butter on rice cake.
2) Place apple slices evenly on top.

Tip — Can sprinkle with raisins, nuts, cinnamon, or ground flax seed.

> ✓ Prep-time: 4 min
> ✓ Cost Factor: $
> ✓ Serves: 1

Chicken Ranch Wrap

This is a flavorful treat you can eat on the go, giving you a slight boost and not weighing you down.

NEED:

- 2 chicken strips, grilled
- Splash of olive oil
- Salt/pepper
- 1 small soft tortilla
- Squirt of Ranch dressing
- 1 small handful of romaine lettuce, shredded

TO DO:

1) Cook chicken strips in a pan on the stove with a little olive oil, salt and pepper.
2) Place warm chicken on tortilla.
3) Squirt a small amount of Ranch dressing.
4) Top with romaine lettuce.

✓ Prep-time: 2 min
✓ Cook-time: about 7 min
✓ Cost Factor: $
✓ Serves: 1

Ground Chicken Meatballs

I know what you're thinking, for a snack? These little balls of joy are high in protein and have fabulous flavor to keep you from crashing. I suggest you make this as a dinner meal with the works (pasta and sauce) and make plenty of meatballs to munch on for leftovers- yes, they are THAT good!

NEED:

- 1 lb ground chicken
- 2 large handfuls Italian breadcrumbs
- 1 egg, beaten
- 2 garlic cloves, finely minced
- 2 handfuls grated parmesan cheese
- Small handful fresh Italian parsley, roughly chopped
- Few dashes of salt/pepper
- Few splashes olive oil

TO DO:

1) Preheat oven to 375°.
2) Mix all ingredients together in a large mixing bowl using your hands — this part can be pretty fun!
3) Using your palm, create balls (little bigger than a golf ball).
4) Lightly brown the meatballs in a pan with a little olive oil on medium heat, gently turning them often (takes about 6 minutes) using two forks or tongs.
5) Transfer to baking sheet and bake for about 10 minutes (or until thoroughly cooked).
6) You can eat them cold or warm, with or without marinara sauce.

- ✓ Prep-time: 8 min
- ✓ Cook-time: under 20 min
- ✓ Cost Factor: $$
- ✓ Serves: 4

Decadent *Dips*

I have eaten more dips in college than anywhere else I have ever been! Dips will play a starring role for you too. Whether studying for a test, hanging out with the roomies, or socializing at parties, I have put together exciting MUST have dips for an occasion. These low cost simple to make dips are delightfully delicious. All the entries are healthy recipes that make people feel comfortable together.

Hummus Dip

I have this in my refrigerator about 24/7. Although hummus is available to buy, it is super simple and easy to make. Earthy and smooth flavors paired with the crunch of your favorite veggie, cracker, or toasted pita bread keeps college munchies under control.

NEED:

- 1 (15 oz) can of chickpeas, drained
- 3-4 scoops of tahini (similar to peanut butter — sold in most grocery stores)
- 1 lemon or lime, juiced
- 2 garlic cloves
- Few pinches of salt
- Few splashes olive oil

TO DO:

1) Add chickpeas, tahini, the juice of one lemon/lime (add a teaspoon of zest, optional), garlic, salt in a blender or food processor and drizzle in olive oil as needed (you want a thick dip consistency).
2) The trick here is to keep tasting and adding more of the ingredients you need. It's all up to your preferences.

Tip — Add red peppers, garlic, or artichoke to your hummus to spice it up. I like to make this on Sunday so I will have it for the week to munch on. It's a great way to get my vegetable servings in.

✓ Prep-time: 10 min
✓ Cost Factor: $

Guacamole Dip

This is a classic dip to have on hand during your years as a student. This delightful dip along with your favorite chips is a great snack to unwind with after a long day of classes.

NEED:

- 2 ripe Haas avocados, mashed
- 1 small tomato, diced
- ½ lime, juiced
- 2 garlic cloves, minced
- Few dashes salt/pepper
- Couple pinches of fresh cilantro (if you have it on hand), chopped

TO DO:

1) Stir in all ingredients in bowl and ta-daaa!

✓ Prep-time: 7 min
✓ Cost Factor: $

Spinach Artichoke Dip

A favorite dip for many! Rich, creamy, tangy, and cheesy are flavors many people often crave. Oh so heavenly! Smother it on chips, crackers or toasted slices of bread.

NEED:

- ½ onion, finely chopped
- 1 scoop of butter
- 1 box of frozen chopped spinach, thawed and drained
- 8 oz sour cream
- 8 oz cream cheese
- 1 jar of marinated artichokes, chopped
- Couple dashes of red pepper flakes (optional)
- 2 large handfuls of shredded, Italian-blend cheese

> ✓ Prep-time: 5 min
> ✓ Cook-time: 8 min
> ✓ Cost Factor: $

TO DO:

1) Sauté onion with butter in a pan until translucent.
2) Add spinach, sour cream, cream cheese, artichoke, and pepper flakes (optional).
3) Stir in all ingredients until creamy.
4) Pour in a microwavable serving bowl and sprinkle cheese on top until melted.
5) Serve warm.

Healthy and Hearty Dip

Light, refreshing, and a zingy flavor taste so good with tortilla chips, crackers, or even just by itself.

NEED:

- 1 (15 oz) can of whole kernel corn, drained
- 1 (15 oz) can of black beans, drained and rinsed
- 1 large handful of cherry tomatoes, sliced in half
- 1 lime, juiced
- Few pinches of fresh cilantro, roughly chopped
- Salt/pepper to taste

TO DO:

1) Toss all ingredients in bowl and lightly mix together.

> ✓ Prep-time: 6 min
> ✓ Cost Factor: $

Buffalo Chicken Dip

Spicy, creamy, and addicting! Taste as if you are eating buffalo chicken wings. Great to munch on with celery sticks, crackers or tortilla chips.

NEED:

- 2 cups of chicken, cooked and finely shredded
- ¾ cup buffalo sauce (may add more/less depending on taste preference)
- 8 oz cream cheese
- ¼ cup Ranch dressing

TO DO:

1) Beat all ingredients together in large bowl.
2) Yep, that's it!

- ✓ Prep-time: 12 min
- ✓ Cost Factor: $

Mexican Dip

This dip is great to make on a Sunday to munch on throughout the week or as a favorite to bring to a dinner party.

NEED:

- 1 (15 oz) can of refried beans
- 2-3 Haas avocados, mashed
- 2 large handfuls of Mexican cheese blend
- 8 oz sour cream
- 1 (16 oz) jar of your favorite salsa
- 1 can of black olives, drained and sliced

TO DO:

1) Preheat oven to 350°.
2) In a deep baking dish, layer the refried beans and evenly spread using back of a spoon.
3) Spread the mashed avocados over the beans and add a thin layer of cheese.
4) Spread the sour cream and layer the salsa on top.
5) Sprinkle cheese on top.
6) Bake until cheese on top is melted.
7) Garnish with sliced black olives.

✓ Prep-time: 10 min
✓ Cook-time: about 7 min
✓ Cost Factor: $$

Cream Cheese and Salsa Dip

That simply is all that it is — cream cheese and salsa. Hands down, it's the world's easiest dip right here! Inexpensive and easy...and great to share with the roomies!

NEED:

- 1 (8 oz) block of Philly cream cheese
- 1 (16 oz) jar of your favorite salsa

TO DO:

1) Place cream cheese on a serving plate.
2) Pour salsa on top.

Tip — Recommend serving with tortilla chips.

✓ Prep-time: 2 min
✓ Cost Factor: $

Super Bowl Dip

When it comes to football season every year, this dip is guaranteed to go FAST and be VICTORIOUS!

NEED:
- 1 lb of ground beef
- 1 (32 oz) box Velveeta cheese
- 1 (10 oz) can Rotel tomatoes, diced

TO DO:
1) Break up ground beef in small chunks in a pan on stove and cook thoroughly.
2) Add the cheese until melted.
3) Stir in the can of Rotel tomatoes.
4) Serve warm with A LOT of chips!

✓ Prep-time: 2 min
✓ Cook-time: about 10 min
✓ Cost Factor: $

Crowd *Pleasers*

What will you bring to tailgates, potlucks, socials and parties? Imagine carrying one of these dishes to an event with a confident smile knowing it's a hit, and that it didn't bust your bank account. All the selections are simple to make, easy to transport and will definitely get conversations rolling. Although I have provided dish variety, you can customize each one, or 'change it up' to suit your group! There are many acceptable choices of cheese, pasta, fruit and veggies.

Italian Pasta Salad

Everyone has his or her own way of doing this dish. My way has color, tang, and my favorite…veggies!

NEED:

- 1 box of rigatoni pasta
- 1 bell pepper (whichever color is on sale)
- 1 small pkg of fresh mixed carrots and broccoli
- 2 big handfuls of parmesan cheese
- Few drizzles of your favorite Italian salad dressing

TO DO:

1) Boil/drain pasta according to box directions.
2) Cut the veggies into thin strips.
3) Combine pasta, veggies, cheese, and dressing in large bowl.
4) Refrigerate.

Tip — the longer it sits, the more flavor.

✓ Prep-time: 15 min
✓ Cook-time: 8 min
✓ Cost Factor: $
✓ Serves: 8-10

Cucumber and Bacon Sandwich

Fresh, crunchy, salty, creamy goodness! This was a request from tailgaters. My friends finally began making it themselves (but not until our senior year). Keep this sandwich chilled.

NEED:

- 1 pkg of turkey bacon
- 2 French or Cuban bread loaves from bakery section
- 8 oz low-fat cream cheese
- Few sprinkles of dill weed
- ¼ onion, thinly sliced
- 1 English cucumber, thinly sliced (it has fewer seeds and more crunch!)
- 2 handfuls of sprouts (I know, some are not a fan — but trust me)

TO DO:

1) Preheat oven to 400°.
2) Bake about 10 slices of bacon (5 pieces for each loaf) and let cool.
3) Slice loaves in half and generously spread cream cheese onto both sides.
4) Sprinkle dill weed and onion over cream cheese.
5) Layer the bacon strips, cucumber and place the sprouts on top.
6) Fold this delicious sandwich and cut into (1½″ slices).

Tip — to keep it together and pretty, place a toothpick in each piece (flag toothpicks add a little something extra to this dish).

✓ Prep-time: 15 min
✓ Cook-time: 12 min
✓ Cost Factor: $$
✓ Serves: 8-10

Marshmallow and Lime Fresh Fruit Salad

My dad and gram's claim-to-fame... this got me eating a lot of fruit as a little girl. Even if you are not big into eating daily servings of fruit, you will this time. The lime adds a fresh tang, which really brings out the flavor of the other fruits in this dish. Having a little marshmallow to go along with each bite brings additional sweetness, color, texture, and flavor.

NEED:

- 2 apples, cut into bite size chunks
- 1 lb of grapes
- 1 pint of strawberries, sliced
- 1 pineapple, cut into bite-size chunks
- 1 can of Clementine oranges with juice
- 1 lime, juiced
- 2 big handfuls of mini marshmallows

✓ Prep-time: 15 min
✓ Cost Factor: $
✓ Serves: 8-10

TO DO:

1) Place fruit in a large (fancy, if you have one) bowl.
2) Add the can of Clementine with the juice.
3) Cut the lime in half and squeeze the juice in (watch for seeds).
4) Gently toss together and add in marshmallows.

Tip — use ANY fresh fruit you have on hand.

Mexican Salad

The sweet from the corn, the spice of the taco seasoning mix, and crunch from the fresh romaine will get people talking about this dish. The varitey of flavors and textures make this dish a hit!

NEED:

- ¾ box of penne pasta
- 3 chicken breasts
- 1 pkg taco seasoning mix
- 2 bunches of romaine lettuce
- 2 tomatoes, diced
- ¼ onion, thinly sliced
- 1 (15 oz) can of drained corn
- 1 (15 oz) can of black beans, drained and rinsed
- 2 large handfuls of Mexican cheese
- Few squirts of your favorite Ranch dressing

TO DO:

1) Boil/drain pasta according to box directions and refrigerate.
2) Cut chicken breast into bite-size. strips, put into large pan on stove and cook with about ½ taco seasoning mix (your call) with a splash of water. Let cool after cooking.
3) Cut romaine lettuce, tomatoes, and onion and place into large bowl.
4) Add in corn, black beans, pasta, chicken, cheese, and Ranch dressing.
5) Toss it all together and serve chilled.

Tip — add a few tortilla chips either crunched up on top or whole chips around the bowl. This adds a little extra crunch and an appealing look to the delicious fiesta.

✓ Prep-time: 20 min
✓ Cook-time: 15 min
✓ Cost Factor: $$
✓ Serves: 5-6

The "Simple Salad"

This salad is a favorite. Growing up, my mom did a similar version once a week. This sharp salad is healthy, fresh, colorful, and good for you!

NEED:

- 4 Roma tomatoes, cut into bite size chunks
- ½ onion, thinly sliced
- 2 cucumbers, thinly sliced
- 1 ball of fresh mozzarella cheese, cut into bite size chunks
- 1 handful of fresh basil leaves, roughly torn
- Few dashes of balsamic vinegar and olive oil
- Salt/pepper to taste

TO DO:

1) Combine all ingredients in bowl.
2) Add vinegar/oil, and salt/pepper.
3) Lightly toss together. Yum-ol-la!

- ✓ Prep-time: 10 min
- ✓ Cost Factor $$
- ✓ Serves: 5-6

Beer Brats and Caramelized Onions

It will be a PARTY in your mouth! With all the decadent different flavors going on, you will smile as you chew. With softened, warm, sweet onions topped on your brat, the thought of any other condiments will not even cross your mind.

NEED:

- 2 packages of beer brats (about 6 in each packet)
- 2 large white onions, sliced
- ½ stick butter
- 2 handfuls brown sugar
- Hoagie rolls (about a dozen)

TO DO:

1) Cook brats thoroughly either on a grill, in the oven, or on the stovetop (no rules!) (usually about 30 minutes).
2) Throw onion, butter, and brown sugar in a pan and simmer on low heat until onions are soft and translucent.
3) Toast hoagie rolls in oven on about 375° for about 8 minutes or until golden.
4) Place your brat on the roll and top with the caramelized onions and its juices. Party on!

✓ Prep-time: 10 min
✓ Cook-time: 30 min
✓ Cost Factor: $
✓ Serves: 8

Orange Cup Sweet Potatoes

This is such a FUN crowd pleaser that will get everyone asking for the recipe. Stylish little orange rind cups filled with creamy warm sweet potatoes and topped with fluffy marshmallows is a head turner. Purely scrumptious! Thank you Aunt Bonnie for your inspiration!

NEED:

- 5 oranges
- 5 medium sweet potatoes
- Couple dashes of cinnamon
- Small handful of brown sugar
- ½ stick butter
- 4 handfuls of mini marshmallows

TO DO:

1) Preheat oven to 400°
2) Cut each orange in half and dig out the middle with a spoon. Leave the rind (cup) looking pretty.
3) Bake sweet potatoes for about an hour or until soft.
4) Scoop out the inside of the sweet potatoes and place in a mixing bowl with cinnamon, brown sugar, butter and a few splashes of juice from the oranges (can add a little bit of zest as well). Mix together until smoothly blended.
5) Replace the sweet potatoes into the orange cups and top with mini marshmallows.
6) Bake in the oven again at 375° for about 15 minutes to get marshmallows golden brown.

Tip — save the scooped out orange to snack on later or to add to your fruit salad.

✓ Prep-time: 25 min
✓ Cook-time: Little over an hr
✓ Cost Factor: $
✓ Serves: 10

Comfort *Foods*

F Feeling a little homesick and missing Mom's cooking? Are you are suffering from a bad breakup? Did you get a 'D' or an 'F' even though you pulled an all nighter? These are times that try a person's appetite. If you feel food will make it better, I have just the dishes to see you through! Sometimes these recipes call for some emotional help from your closest friends to help you get out of your funk. Enjoy eating them together.

Viva La Difference Lasagna

This is a popular request among my friends and family and every time I make it, it tastes a little different, which intensifies the thrill of making it. Whether it is the intermingling of flavors, or simply that full satisfaction you feel after consuming it, this dish will effectively gratify your every mood.

NEED:

- 1 lb of ground chicken
- 1 (25 oz) jar of favorite marinara sauce
- 2 eggs
- 15 oz container of ricotta cheese (can substitute cottage cheese- save $!)
- 4 cups of Italian cheese mix or just mozzarella
- 2 handfuls of fresh, flat-leaf Italian parsley, roughly chopped
- Few dashes salt/pepper
- Precooked lasagna flat noodles

TO DO:

1) Preheat oven to 375°.
2) Cook ground chicken in a pan, break up to bite size chunks and stir in marinara sauce.
3) Combine 2 eggs, ricotta cheese, 2 cups of cheese, 1 handful of parsley, and salt/pepper in a bowl.
4) Start layering! In a 9x13" baking pan, 1st put in chicken and sauce, 2nd layer noodles, 3rd cheese mixture, 4th a thin layer of sprinkled cheese. Repeat until you use up all ingredients and finish with layer of cheese.
5) Cover baking pan with alumium foil and bake for 1 hour, take foil off for the last 10 minutes.
6) Allow to cool for 5 minutes before cutting, to prevent oozing!
7) Top with fresh parsley.

> ✓ Prep-time: 15 min
> ✓ Cook-time: 1 hr total
> ✓ Cost Factor: $$
> ✓ Serves: 8

Tuna Melt

A tuna mixture spread generously over a piece of crispy toast or roll and topped with melted Swiss cheese is a great, reassuring dish and goes great with a bowl of your favorite veggie soup.

NEED:

- 2 (6 oz) cans of tuna
- ¼ onion, finely chopped
- 2 celery stalks, finely chopped (optional)
- Few scoops mayonnaise
- 2 squirts of mustard (any style)
- Salt/pepper to taste
- Few slices of Swiss cheese
- Few pieces of toast or roll

> ✓ Prep-time: 7 min
> ✓ Cook-time: 2 min
> ✓ Cost factor: $
> ✓ Serves: 2-3

TO DO:

1) Drain tuna cans and place in large bowl.
2) Mix in onion, celery, mayo, mustard, and salt and pepper.
3) Place tuna mixture on toasted bread or roll.
4) Put 1 or 2 slices of cheese on each piece of toast and nuke in the microwave until lightly melted.

Classy Grilled Cheese

This is a new dolled up version of your typical grilled cheese sandwich.

NEED:

- 1 small scoop butter
- 2 slices of bread
- 1 small scoop Dijon mustard
- 2 slices American cheese
- 2 slices ham
- ½ small tomato, thinly sliced

✓ Prep-time: 5 min
✓ Cook-time: 6 min
✓ Cost Factor: $
✓ Serves: 1

TO DO:

1) Spread a thin layer of butter on both sides of bread.
2) Spread Dijon mustard on insides of bread, layer with: cheese, ham, and tomato slices.
3) Place sandwich in pan on medium/low heat (you can use a spatula to press down on sandwich to speed up cooking-time).
4) Cook evenly on both sides until golden brown and cheese has melted inside.

Peanut Butter and Jelly French Toast

This is a jazzed up version of the traditional boring PB&J. On a cold Sunday morning or a late night snack, this is just the treat.

NEED:

- 1 egg
- Splash of milk
- 2 slices of bread
- 2 scoops peanut butter
- 1 scoop jelly
- 1 scoop of butter
- Maple syrup

✓ Prep-time: 8 min
✓ Cook-time: 5 min
✓ Cost Factor: $
✓ Serves: 1

TO DO:

1) In a bowl beat the egg and splash of milk.
2) Make your normal PB&J sandwich and then soak both sides in the egg and milk mixture.
3) Place the PB&J sandwich in a pan with melted butter on medium heat.
4) Cook for about 2 minutes on both sides or until golden brown.
5) Drizzle a little bit of maple syrup and enjoy!

Creamy Dreamy Mashies

This dish will top your mom's traditional Thanksgiving mashed potatoes. With the rich and velvety flavors this dish has to offer, it will soothe your worries and put you on cloud nine.

NEED:

- 4 potatoes (Idaho, Yukon, etc..), whichever are cheapest
- 2 large scoops sour cream
- 2 handfuls shredded cheddar cheese
- 2 scoops butter
- 2 scoops mayonnaise
- Few pinches chopped chives or parsley
- Bacon bits (optional)
- Salt/pepper to taste

> ✓ Prep-time: 5 min
> ✓ Cook-time: 10 min
> ✓ Cost Factor: $
> ✓ Serves: 4

TO DO:

1) Wash, peel, dice and place potatoes into large pot of boiling salted water.
2) Drain immediately after boiling 10 minutes.
3) Throw all the other ingredients in the same pot (add more of anything if needed) and mash away! This part gives you the opportunity to relieve any negative tension…mash mash mash! Then enjoy!

O'Shea's Famous Clam Chowder

This recipe was created by my grandfather, Thomas Shea, and was served in my grandparent's restaurant O'Shea's for 22 years. I think it's safe to say this is my all time favorite soup! Thanks grandpa!!

NEED:

- 5 slices of bacon, diced
- 2 celery stalks, chopped
- 1 medium onion, diced
- 2 tbsp flour
- 1 tbsp butter
- 1 (6.5 oz) can of clams
- 1 (8 oz) bottle of clam juice
- 4 medium potatoes, boiled and diced
- Few dashes salt/pepper
- ¼ tsp thyme
- ¾ pint half and half

> ✓ Prep-time: 13 min
> ✓ Cook-time: 25 min
> ✓ Cost Factor: $$
> ✓ Serves: 6

TO DO:

1) Cook bacon in a large pot: then cook celery and onion in bacon fat until softened, drain bacon fat.
2) Mix flour and butter with a whisk in a small saucepan to make a roux (like a paste), cook for 5 minutes.
3) Add roux, clams, clam juice, potatoes, salt/pepper and thyme to bacon, celery and onion. Let cook for about 15 minutes on medium heat.
4) Warm half and half first, then add to pot.
5) If mixture starts to separate, add a little more half and half at the last minute.

Fancy Mac and Cheese

Cheese is just the cure! Warm and gooey cheesy goodness with chunks of salty pancetta and fresh Italian parsley will turn your frown upside down.

NEED:
- ½ box of Penne pasta
- 2 large handfuls of sharp cheddar cheese
- 2 scoops of butter
- Few slices of pancetta or bacon, cooked and chopped in bite sizes
- Salt/pepper to taste
- 1 handful of fresh Italian parsley, roughly chopped

TO DO:
1) Boil/drain penne pasta according to directions on box and return to pot.
2) Add cheese, butter, pancetta, salt and pepper, and mix together.
3) Top with parsley and enjoy!

- ✓ Prep-time: 15 min
- ✓ Cook-time: 10 min
- ✓ Cost Factor: $
- ✓ Serves: 3

Dropping
Freshman 15

I know I can't speak for everyone, but most will agree, late night pizza runs, fast food oink-outs as well as 'guzzle-fuzzelments' of certain beverages can grow new fat on your body faster than you can say Bacon Butt Beer Burger backward. Toward the end of my first year in college I realized the saying, Freshman 15, was becoming a reality. Eating healthy food in moderate amounts is a lifestyle choice you need to make now. You and your roomies will have fun with these easy to prepare dishes. The goal of this chapter is to keep your body trim, your wallet fat and your taste buds satisfied! Ohhhhhh-yeaaaa!

My personal tips when keeping the pounds down:

➤ Drink a glass of water before any meal.

➤ Slow down! Sit down while you eat and enjoy the ingredients you're consuming.

➤ Don't skip breakfast.

➤ Try not to eat after 7:30 p.m.

➤ Don't load up on the carbs.

➤ Remember portion and control, save some for the next day.

➤ Focus on veggies and fruits.

➤ Eating a few nuts (almonds, walnuts) before a meal will encourage you to eat less.

➤ Exercise — I know, DUH! But I just had to write it ☺

Veggie Soup

I know, soups can be pretty boring and the thought of making them is simply scary, but just give this one a try because it is SUPER SIMPLE! It can be a great meal or an afternoon snack and it's a tasty leftover.

NEED:

- 4 celery stalks, finely chopped
- 4 carrots, finely chopped
- ½ onion, finely chopped
- A splash of olive oil
- 1 small head of cabbage, thinly sliced
- 1 large handful of mushrooms, thinly sliced
- Salt/pepper to taste
- 1 (32 oz) box of vegetable stock

TO DO:

1) Place celery, carrots, and onion into a large pot with olive oil and cook until softened for about 8 minutes on medium heat.
2) Add cabbage, mushrooms, and salt and pepper.
3) Simmer for about 10 minutes then add vegetable stock.

- ✓ Prep-time: 20 min
- ✓ Cook-time: 40 min
- ✓ Cost Factor: $
- ✓ Serves: 6

Strawberry-Banana Smoothie

Think: refreshing, light and fruity with a hint of creamy dreaminess in the background. Whenever I had early morning, summer school classes, this was a refreshing treat to motivate me to get out of bed. This low-fat cool drink was enjoyable to sip on while strolling to class. It was just enough to keep my focus and keep my stomach from growling.

NEED:

- 1 banana
- 1 handful of (fresh or frozen) strawberries
- 1 large scoop of low fat plain yogurt
- 1 handful of ice
- Either a splash of skim milk or fruit juice

TO DO:

1) Super easy- ready for this? Put everything in a blender and unify! YUM!

Tip — a dash of vanilla extract adds additional flavor and sweetness. Also, for really hot days, don't be shy on extra ice.

- ✓ Prep-time: 5 min
- ✓ Cost Factor: $
- ✓ Serves: 1

Pear and Gorgonzola Salad

A smooth creamy salad, a second favorite of mine. This is another super easy and healthy salad that will keep your stature lean and energy level high. Who would have thought salads could be so exciting?

NEED:

- 3 handfuls of either fresh spinach or mixed greens
- 1 pear, thinly sliced
- 1 small handful of gorgonzola cheese crumbled
- ¼ onion, thinly sliced
- 1 small handful nuts (walnuts, almonds or pecans), roughly chopped
- Your favorite vinaigrette dressing or balsamic vinaigrette and olive oil

TO DO:

1) Add all ingredients to a large bowl and toss together — Yum-ol-la!

✓ Prep-time: 10 min
✓ Cost Factor: $
✓ Serves: 2

Spinach Apple Salad

My all time favorite salad!! I've turned a lot of my girlfriends onto this healthy, greeny goodness. Not only is this salad high in fiber and vitamins, it has just the right amount of sweetness and crunch to satisfy your palate.

NEED:

- 3 large handfuls of fresh spinach
- 1 Fuji or gala apple, thinly sliced
- 1 large handful of plump raisins
- 1 small handful of nuts (walnuts, almonds or pecans), roughly chopped
- Your favorite vinaigrette dressing or balsamic vinaigrette and olive oil

TO DO:

1) Toss spinach, sliced apples, raisins, walnuts and dressing in a large bowl (use your own judgment with the amount — remember less is more). Couldn't be easier, huh?

Tip — Because this salad already has a lot of flavor, I usually keep the salad dressing in a side cup and dip my fork in each time before stabbing my bites. By doing this, I use about half of what I would use if dressing were poured on.

✓ Prep-time: 10 min
✓ Cost Factor: $
✓ Serves: 2

Strawberry Feta Salad

Another tasty and healthy salad! This is a wonderful summer-time favorite pared with just the right ingredients to get you swimsuit ready.

NEED:

- 3 handfuls of either fresh spinach or mixed greens
- 1 large handful fresh strawberries, sliced
- 1 small handful of feta cheese crumbled
- 1 small handful nuts (walnuts, almonds or pecans), roughly chopped
- ¼ onion, thinly sliced
- Your favorite vinaigrette dressing (strawberry) or balsamic vinaigrette and olive oil

TO DO:

1) Combine the goods in large bowl and enjoy!

✓ Prep-time: 10 min
✓ Cost Factor: $
✓ Serves: 2

Grilled Turkey Burgers

These lean burgers beat the normal greasy beef burgers by a long shot.   Full of great earthy flavors, this burger gets an A+ for being a great source of lean protein. Great for lunch, dinner, and can be crumbled up in your breakfast eggs or paired with your favorite salad.

✓ Prep-time: 10 min
✓ Cook-time: 10 min
✓ Cost Factor: $
✓ Serves: 4

NEED:

- 1 lb ground turkey
- ¼ onion, finely chopped
- 1 egg (the glue that holds the patties together)
- ½ tablespoon thyme
- ½ tablespoon sage
- Few dashes of salt/pepper
- Ketchup
- American cheese slices (optional- watching the calories? leave it out)

TO DO:

1) Combine ground turkey, onion, egg, thyme, sage, salt/pepper, and a squirt of ketchup (keeps it moist) in large bowl.
2) Mix all ingredients using your hands (take off all rings!) and get down and dirty with it! Form patties about the size of your palm.
3) Cook patties about 5 minutes on each side (depends on thickness) using a George Foreman Grill, a "real" grill, or a stovetop pan.
4) Add cheese at last minute if desired.

Grilled Shrimp and Asparagus

Succulent shrimp served over roasted asparagus with a citrus punch is a quick fix to your hunger needs. This low-calorie, fresh-flavored meal is easy to prepare before a night exam. Already rich with flavors, not much is needed to satisfy your taste buds.

NEED:

- 1 bundle of asparagus with though ends cut off
- Few drizzles olive oil
- Salt/pepper to taste
- About 10 shrimp (if you can't get fresh, frozen will do)
- 1 clove garlic, minced
- 1 lemon

> ✓ Prep-time: 5 min
> ✓ Cook-time: 20 min
> ✓ Cost Factor: $$
> ✓ Serves: 2

TO DO:

1) Preheat oven to 375°.
2) Coat asparagus on baking sheet with a generous amount of olive oil and salt/pepper and bake for 20 minutes.
3) Cook garlic in a pan on low heat with olive oil for about 7 minutes (don't let it burn because it becomes bitter — gross!).
4) Season shrimp with salt/pepper and add to pan with the garlic.
5) Cook shrimp (about 3 minutes on each side or until pink).
6) Slice lemon in half and squeeze juice all over asparagus.
7) Place shrimp on top of asparagus and squeeze the other half of lemon on top (can add zest of lemon as well).

Spaghetti Squash

This is a super easy and light dish not many students know about! A great substitute for your pasta cravings! My sister, Jenni, has turned me on to the wonderful world of squash... Thanks!

NEED:

- 1 spaghetti squash
- 1 small scoop of butter
- Few dashes of salt/pepper
- Few scoops of spaghetti sauce (optional)

> ✓ Prep-time: 2 min
> ✓ Cook-time: about 40 min
> ✓ Cost Factor: $
> ✓ Serves: 4

TO DO:

1) Preheat oven to 375°.
2) Cut squash in half lengthwise and scoop out seeds.
3) Place cut side down in baking pan with a few splashes of water.
4) Flip squash over, use a fork and scrape it out (looks like angel hair pasta).
5) Stir in butter, salt/pepper, and spaghetti sauce (optional).

The Any White Fish Dish

You know what they say, fish is brain food! I always tried to eat fish before a final (it was a mental thing...being EXTRA prepared). This is a great way to cook up any white fish of your choice. The ingredients I suggest will add great flavor to each and every bite.

NEED:

- 1 lb of your favorite white fish (sole, grouper, cod, sea bass, tilapia, etc...)
- Few dashes of olive oil
- Salt/pepper
- 1 lemon
- 2 Scoops capers
- Splashes of white wine or Marsala (optional)
- Few sprinkles of fresh Italian parsley, chopped

> ✓ Prep-time: 8 min
> ✓ Cook-time: 20-30 (depends on thickness of fish)
> ✓ Cost Factor: $$ (depends on choice of fish)
> ✓ Serves: 2

TO DO:

1) Preheat oven to 350°.
2) Place fish on baking pan and coat with olive oil (drizzle extra on pan), salt/pepper, ½ juice of lemon, capers, and few splashes of white wine/Marsala.
3) Serve with other half of lemon juice, capers, and parsley. YUM!

Healthy Eggy Goodness

This veggie filled, hunger stopper, protein-filled dish is just the trick for maintaining your trim figure. After eating this for breakfast with a piece of whole-wheat toast, picking on junk food doesn't cross my mind. ☺

NEED:

- ¼ small onion, finely chopped
- 1 large handful of spinach
- Spash of olive oil
- 2 slices of chopped turkey bacon (optional, but adds extra flavor and protein)
- 3 egg whites
- 1 slice of your favorite cheese (again, optional)
- ½ small tomato, diced
- Few dashes of salt/pepper

TO DO:

1) Throw onion, spinach, and bacon in a pan with olive oil.
2) Simmer over medium/low heat until soft.
3) Add eggs and cheese to the other ingredients and cook until done.
4) Transfer onto plate and top with tomatoes and salt/pepper. YUM!

> ✓ Prep-time: 7 min
> ✓ Cook-time: 8 min
> ✓ Cost Factor: $
> ✓ Serves: 1-2

Yogurt Burst

This can be a great breakfast or snack. This light, smooth and healthy dish will allow you to get some of your fruits and dairy servings in for the day.

NEED:

- 2 scoops of low fat vanilla or plain yogurt
- 1 small handful of strawberries, sliced
- ½ orange, bite size chunks
- ½ banana, sliced
- ½ apple, sliced
- 1 small handful of granola or a hearty cereal

✓ Prep-time: 12 min
✓ Cost Factor: $
✓ Serves: 1

TO DO:

1) Combine yogurt and fruit in a bowl.
2) Sprinkle with granola.

Tip — any of your favorite fruit (hopefully on sale) can be added to this. Nuts can also be added for an extra crunch.

Pinchin' Pennies

Regardless of where your college money comes from, you want to save money on buying food and beverages. You probably get lectures from Mom and Dad on how to stretch the budget (your weekly or monthly allowance). 2009, the year this book went to publication, was a hard year financially for most families. Buying the freshest fruits and vegetables on sale, or with coupons is a smart thing to do. I have included healthy, easy to prepare meals that offer solid nutritional value.

> "
> *If you watch over the pennies of your food budget, the savings could end up as dollars of enjoyment.*
> "

New Orleans Rib Sticker

Full of fiber, flavor, protein, and will keep your tummy content. Another dish that will allow for PLENTY of leftovers!

NEED:

- 2 cups rice, your favorite one on sale will do
- 1 pkg of kielbasa or some type of sausage on sale, diced
- Few splashes of olive oil
- 1 small onion, finely diced
- 1 bell pepper (any color — perhaps the one on sale?), finely diced
- 1 (8 oz) can of tomato sauce
- 1 (15 oz) can of red beans

TO DO:

1) Prepare rice in pot according to package directions.
2) Cook sausage or kielbasa in large pan.
3) Add olive oil, onion, and pepper and cook on medium/low heat for a few minutes.
4) Stir in tomato paste and beans together.
5) Throw in the cooked rice and enjoy!

> ✓ Prep-time: 12 min
> ✓ Cook-time: 15 min
> ✓ Cost Factor: $
> ✓ Serves: 5

Tuna Pasta

Gives you energy, protein, and satisfaction for those on a serious budget! This recipe provides plenty of leftovers.

NEED:

- 1 box of your favorite pasta (penne, rigatoni)
- 2-3 (6 oz) cans of tuna (light and in water)
- ½ small onion, finely diced
- Few celery stalks, finely chopped (optional)
- Few scoops of mayonnaise
- Salt/pepper to taste

TO DO:

1) Boil/drain pasta according to box directions.
2) Mix together tuna (don't forget to drain the juice), onion, celery, mayo, and salt/pepper in a large bowl.
3) Add the pasta, toss together and refrigerate.

> ✓ Prep-time: 8 min
> ✓ Cook-time: 10 min
> ✓ Cost Factor: $
> ✓ Serves: 5

BBQ Chicken Legs and Baked Beans

Chicken legs always seem like a great deal. You can buy about 10 for around $5 what a steal! Add some BBQ sauce and some beans and there you have a complete meal!

NEED:

- Chicken legs (as many as you want or best deal)
- BBQ sauce (enough to marinate)
- 1 (15 oz) can of baked beans

TO DO:

1) Coat chicken legs in a bowl or zip-lock bag with generous amount of BBQ sauce and let marinate (for however long time permits).
2) Cook legs and turn often in an 375° oven, or on a grill.
3) Add more BBQ sauce if needed.
4) Heat baked beans and serve.

> ✓ Prep-time: 5 min
> ✓ Cook-time: 20 min
> ✓ Cost Factor: $
> ✓ Serves: 4 (how hungry?)

Ramen Tuna

What's a cheap dish without RAMEN noodles?? Cheesy. Cheap. Quick.

NEED:

- 2 pkg Raman noodles (seasoning optional)
- 2 (6 oz) cans of tuna
- 8 oz cream cheese

TO DO:

1) Boil/drain noodles according to package.
2) Drain tuna juice, mix tuna, noodles and cream cheese together in large bowl.

> ✓ Prep-time: 2 min
> ✓ Cook-time: 7 min
> ✓ Cost Factor: $
> ✓ Serves: 4

Erin's Ramen P-a-a-r-t-a-y

Ok, one more Ramen dish. Last one, promise! It's a winner!

NEED:

- 3 pkg Ramen Noodles (use one chicken seasoning packet)
- 1 (15 oz) can corn, drained
- 1 (6 oz) can tuna, drained
- 1 handful Colby-Jack cheese (or whatever is in the refrigerator)

TO DO:

1) Boil/drain noodles according to package directions.
2) Toss all ingredients together in a large bowl.

> ✓ Prep-time: 2 min
> ✓ Cook-time: 7 min
> ✓ Cost Factor: $
> ✓ Serves: 4

Chicken Spaghetti

Yuuuummmmmy and CHEAP. Enough said! ☺

NEED:

- ½ box of pasta (angel hair presents best)
- 1 lb of ground chicken
- 1(25 oz) jar of spaghetti sauce
- 1 handful parmesan cheese (optional)

TO DO:

1) Boil/drain pasta according to box directions.
2) Cook ground chicken thoroughly in a large pan and break into chunks.
3) Add sauce, pasta and sprinkle parmesan cheese.
4) Mix and slurp!

> ✓ Prep-time: 2 min
> ✓ Cook-time: 10 min
> ✓ Cost Factor: $
> ✓ Serves: 4

Pasta Meat Salad

It covers all the food groups, while not breaking the bank!

NEED:

- 1 box pasta (Rigatoni works well)
- ½ lb ground beef/chicken/turkey
- ½ cup salsa
- 1 bunch of romaine lettuce, sliced
- Handful of shredded cheese (cheddar, Mexican blend)

TO DO:

1) Boil/drain pasta according to box directions and let cool.
2) Cook ground beef thoroughly breaking into chunks and let cool.
3) Add pasta, meat, salsa, lettuce, and cheese in a bowl.
4) Toss together and enjoy!

> ✓ Prep-time: 2 min
> ✓ Cook-time: 10 min
> ✓ Cost Factor: $
> ✓ Serves: 4

Homemade Chili

This meal is a favorite of my Aunt Colleen, who claims this dish will last for three to four days. Hearty and satisfying goodies all stuffed in one pot! mmm… The amount of ingredients may seem lengthy, but hey… cans are inexpensive!

NEED:

- 1 lb ground meat/turkey/chicken
- Few splashes of olive oil
- 1 onion, finely diced
- 1 green bell pepper, finely diced
- 1 (15 oz) can kidney beans
- 1 (15 oz) can chili beans
- 1 (6 oz) can tomato paste
- 1 (15 oz) can crushed tomatoes
- Few dashes chili powder (up to you!)
- Shredded cheddar cheese
- Sour cream

✓ Prep-time: 10 min
✓ Cook-time: about 20 min
✓ Cost Factor: $
✓ Serves: 8-10

TO DO:

1) Cook ground meat in large pot on medium heat and break into bite-size chunks.
2) Add olive oil, onion, and bell pepper. Cook until softened.
3) Add all the canned ingredients and chili powder.
4) Cook on low to allow all the flavors to marry.
5) To serve, sprinkle shredded cheddar cheese and top with a scoop of sour cream.

Date Night
Dinners

Whether it's your significant other's birthday, Valentine's Day, or any other important day in your relationship, it is wise to have a celebratory meal plan. These are occasions you want to spend time and money on, so you can impress one you care about. Picnic style, candlelight style, or just hangin-out style, these dishes will make your date feel appreciated!

Shrimp Scampi

People LOVE this dish! Your dinner guest may think you slaved in the kitchen all day. Little do they know…

NEED:

- Few splashes of Marsala or white wine
- 1 carton of Shiitake mushrooms, roughly chopped
- ½ box of angel hair pasta
- Few dashes of extra virgin olive oil
- 3 garlic cloves, minced
- Few splashes of half and half
- 1 bag of frozen shrimp (about 15-25), peeled with tails on, thawed
- Salt/pepper to taste
- Few dashes of red pepper flakes
- 2 large handfuls of grated parmesan cheese
- Small handful of fresh Italian parsley, roughly chopped

> ✓ Prep-time: 10 min
> ✓ Cook-time: 15 min
> ✓ Cost Factor: $$
> ✓ Serves: 3-4

TO DO:

1) Pour the wine in a bowl and toss in mushrooms to absorb flavor.
2) Boil/drain pasta according to box directions.
3) Combine olive oil and garlic in a large pan on medium/low heat.
4) Cook until garlic is soft (make sure it doesn't turn brown! — it will taste bitter).
5) Add a little of the half and half and the wine soaked mushrooms.
6) Throw in the shrimp (they cook fast! Reduce heat to low).
7) Add cooked pasta, the rest of the half and half, and few more splashes of wine (if needed).
8) Mix in salt/pepper, red pepper flakes, cheese, and a drizzle of olive oil.
9) Garnish with parsley on top and WOW…
   Masterpiece!

* Could serve with: salad and toasted, Italian rustic bread.

Ground Turkey Meatloaf

Guys can't seem to get enough of this stuff! This is a healthier version of the traditional meatloaf and is just as flavorful and moist, but with fewer calories. Classic American favorite!

NEED:

- 1 lb of ground turkey
- ½ large onion, finely chopped
- 1 red pepper, finely chopped
- 1 large handful of bread crumbs
- 1 egg, beaten
- Few drizzles of olive oil
- Salt/pepper to taste
- Small handful of fresh Italian parsley, roughly chopped
- Couple squirts of ketchup

✓ Prep-time: 10 min
✓ Cook-time: 35-45 min
✓ Cost Factor: $
✓ Serves: 4

TO DO:

1) Preheat oven to 350°.
2) Combine all ingredients in a large mixing bowl and mix with your hands (take off your rings...it can get pretty messy!).
3) Form a loaf and place in center of baking pan.
4) Drizzle ketchup on top.

*Could serve with: baked potatoes and fresh, steamed broccoli.

Rosemary Orange Roasted Chicken

This is a dish I make at least once a month. Earthy and citrus scents fill the kitchen allowing your guest to experience a mouthwatering entrance. The moist chicken allows for great leftovers to get creative with.

NEED:

- Few drizzles olive oil
- 4 garlic cloves, minced
- 2 tbsp rosemary
- 1 tbsp thyme
- ½ tbsp sage
- Generous amount of salt/pepper
- 2 oranges, sliced
- 1 whole chicken (with liver and gizzards out!-eww!)
- 2 scoops butter

✓ Prep-time: 20 min
✓ Cook-time: 20 min per pound
✓ Cost Factor: $
✓ Serves: 4

TO DO:

1) Preheat oven to 350°.
2) Using a mortar (if you don't have a mortar, use a coffee mug and the back of a thick utensil) pulverize olive oil, garlic, rosemary, thyme, sage, salt/pepper, and a squeeze of juice from one orange and a ½ tbsp of zest (grate the peel of orange).
3) Mash all ingredients together, forming a thick paste.
4) Rub half of the paste all over chicken.
5) Put one sliced orange inside of chicken.
6) Melt butter and a drizzle of olive oil in a large pan (helps the butter from burning) and add the chicken; cook on medium/high heat.
7) Keep turning the chicken to get it evenly golden brown on all sides.
8) Transport chicken to a deep baking pan or a roaster.
9) Use the other half of paste and rub on chicken.
10) Place the other thinly sliced orange on top of chicken, spreading evenly.
11) Cover with aluminum foil and bake.

*Could serve with: wild rice and steamed green beans.

Red Pepper and Dill Salmon

We need our brain food fish! I have many friends who are scared to fix fish for any reason. Come on you guys, get over it, and get familiar with your fishy friends!

NEED:

- Light drizzle of olive oil
- 1 lb salmon filet
- ½ red pepper, thinly sliced
- 2 dashes dill weed
- Few dashes of salt/pepper
- 1 small scoop butter

✓ Prep-time: 10 min
✓ Cook-time: about 25 min
✓ Cost Factor: $$
✓ Serves: 3

TO DO:

1) Preheat oven to 350°.
2) Drizzle a little olive oil in a baking pan so salmon won't stick.
3) Place salmon in baking pan.
4) Evenly sprinkle red peppers, dill weed, salt/pepper, and small (pea-size) chunks of butter.

* Could serve with: sweet potatoes and fresh salad.

BBQ Chicken Pizza

A sweet, cheesy, and tangy pizza is always a favorite for college students. It sure beats late night greasy pizza from the pizza joint!

NEED:

- 2 chicken breasts, diced into small chunks
- Few squirts of BBQ sauce (honey flavor is a favorite)
- 2 thin pizza crusts
- 4 handfuls of Mozzarella cheese, shredded
- ¼ onion, finely chopped

TO DO:

1) Preheat oven to 450°.
2) Cut chicken breasts into small bite size chunks and mix with BBQ sauce.
3) Cook chicken either in a pan or on the grill.
4) Spread BBQ sauce on pizza crust using the back of a spoon.
5) Add a thin layer of cheese.
6) Sprinkle onions on pizza.
7) Distribute chicken on crust evenly.
8) Top with remaining cheese.

*Could serve with: a fresh salad and corn on the cob.

- ✓ Prep-time: 8 min
- ✓ Cook-time: 10 min
- ✓ Cost Factor: $
- ✓ Serves: 4

Pork Chops Smothered in Caramelized Onions

Lean and tender pork chops topped with sweet and savory soft onions. This makes for a tasty leftover treat. This dish will definitely impress!

NEED:

- 1 large onion, thinly sliced
- 1 large handful of brown sugar
- Few scoops of butter
- 4 (4 oz) center-cut pork chops
- Salt/pepper
- Few dashes olive oil

✓ Prep-time: 10 min
✓ Cook-time: 20 min
✓ Cost Factor: $$
✓ Serves: 4

TO DO:

1) Throw in onion, brown sugar, and butter in a pan.
2) Cook on low heat until onions are soft and translucent.
3) Tenderize pork chops by placing them in a thick zip-lock bag (or between two pieces of plastic wrap with a few drops of water on both sides to prevent pastic from breaking) and pound them with a meat tenderizer until they are relatively thin. If you don't have that, use anything flat and heavy (brick, cast iron skillet, textbook).
4) Season pork with salt/pepper.
5) Place in pan with olive oil on medium heat, flipping frequently.
6) Cook completely until golden brown.
7) Serve pork chops topped with caramelized onions and it's juices.

*Could serve with: mashed potatoes and roasted asparagus.

Veal Scaloppini

The name itself sounds impressive and oh so fancy! Tender veal lightly breaded and topped with lemon juice and capers is a fancy dinner for your date.

NEED:

- 1 lb of lean veal cutlets (can substitute in chicken breasts)
- 3 large handfuls of flour
- 2 eggs, beaten
- 3 large handfuls of Italian breadcrumbs
- Olive oil, enough to coat the pan with a thin layer
- 2 lemons, cut in wedges
- 3 scoops of capers
- Balsamic vinegar (optional)

TO DO:

1) I recommend pounding (tenderize) the veal by placing it in a zip-lock bag and pounding it with something heavy (a brick?) to thin it out slightly, but you don't have to.
2) Line up 3 small bowls in the following order: 1st bowl flour, 2nd bowl beaten eggs, and 3rd bowl Italian breadcrumbs.
3) Take each piece of veal and dip/coat it in each bowl in assembly-line style.
4) Cook veal in a large pan with olive oil on medium heat until golden brown on both sides.
5) Place on paper towel to absorb excess oil.
6) Serve with fresh-squeezed lemon juice on top and a few capers with each bite. Try dipping veal in a little balsamic vinegar. Mmmm my favorite!

* Could serve with: lightly buttered pasta and sautéed spinach.

- ✓ Prep-time: 12 min
- ✓ Cook-time: 15-20 min
- ✓ Cost Factor: $$$
- ✓ Serves: 4

Steak Stir-Fry

This steak stir-fry is electrifying and is quick to whip up, so no excuses!

NEED:

- ½ lb beef strips (lean)
- Few splashes olive oil
- 2 garlic cloves, finely minced
- 1 small bundle of broccoli, bite-size chunks
- 1 handful baby carrots, cut in half lengthwise
- About ½ cup soy sauce (reduced sodium) and/or teriyaki sauce (mixing both is tasty!)
- 2 small handfuls bean sprouts
- 2 small handfuls snow peas

✓ Prep-time: 15 min
✓ Cook-time: 15 min
✓ Cost Factor: $$
✓ Serves: 2

TO DO:

1) Place beef and few splashes of soy sauce in a bowl or zip-lock bag to marinate while you chop vegetables.
2) Drizzle two splashes of olive oil and add beef in a large pan.
3) Brown beef on both sides.
4) Add garlic, broccoli, carrots, and a few splashes of soy sauce. Cook on medium/low covered for a few minutes to soften.
5) Lastly, add bean sprouts, snow peas and more soy sauce/olive oil if needed.
6) Toss together in pan and cook on low until vegetables are as tender as you want.

*Could serve with: Chinese noodles or brown rice.

Dorm
Dishes

During my freshman year in the dorm, I found microwave cooking to be a little rough. Factory prepared frozen dinners seemed to taste the same. There was usually a processed slab of meat with gravy and a green mushy vegetable. Yuck! After a while I wanted to engage in creative cooking as well as relieve a little stress, so I decided to experiment with my little black box.

Some things to keep in mind:

- Always use a microwave-safe cooking dish (no metal, people!)
- When handling raw meat, same kitchen rules still apply! Run to the bathroom and thoroughly wash hands!
- Microwaves give off radiation, so try not to hang out right in front of it.
- All microwaves cook a little differently, so my specified time may not be yours
- Try to avoid putting plastic in the microwave (plastic wrap, plastic bowls) all these new studies say it's bad news… cancer?

Hotdog and Baked Beans

Who would have thought you could have BBQ flavors in a small, stuffy dorm room?

NEED:
- ½ (15 oz) can baked beans
- 1 hot dog (or try a turkey dog...they taste just as good!)
- 1 hot dog bun

TO DO:
1) Open can of baked beans, pour in bowl, heat up for about 3 minutes.
2) Place hotdog on paper towel and nuke for about 30 seconds.
3) Serve with hotdog in bun and spoon in some baked beans.

> ✓ Prep-time: 3 min
> ✓ Cook-time: Under 4 min
> ✓ Cost Factor: $
> ✓ Serves: 1

Quesadilla

This is a really quick dish that always hits the spot!

NEED:
- 2 soft taco shells (healthy? Try whole wheat)
- Few scoops salsa
- Handful of cooked ham or turkey (I like using deli meat for this), diced
- Handful of shredded cheese (of your choice- Mexican blend works well!)

TO DO:
1) Lay one soft taco shell flat on a plate.
2) Evenly sprinkle salsa, ham/turkey, and cheese.
3) Nuke for about 30 seconds (until cheese is barely melted).
4) Place the other taco shell directly on top and cook for about another 30 seconds.

> ✓ Prep-time: 5 min
> ✓ Cook-time: about 1 min
> ✓ Cost Factor: $
> ✓ Serves: 1

Shrimp and Grits

I know what you're thinking...grits and shrimp?!? Humm! I didn't experience morning cheese grits until college, and if done right, they are delicious! I got the idea to pair grits with shrimp for a lunch or dinner after dining at a 5 Star restaurant in NYC (who would've thought?)

NEED:

- 1 serving of grits
- 1 scoop of butter
- 1 large handful of shredded cheese (American or Cheddar)
- Salt/pepper to taste
- About 8 shrimp (if frozen, let thaw)

✓ Prep-time: 5 min
✓ Cook-time: about 4 min
✓ Cost Factor: $
✓ Serves: 1

TO DO:

1) Follow microwave instructions for grits.
2) Mix in butter, cheese, and salt.
3) Season shrimp with salt/pepper on both sides and nuke (about 1½ minutes) on one side and flip and do the same on the other side (cook until pink on both sides).
4) Serve on a plate or a bowl with the shrimp placed on top of the grits.

White Fish with Cheesy Broccoli and a Baked Potato

*This is a meal most people wouldn't think could be cooked in a microwave. Surprise!
Simple, healthy, hearty, and quick are the words of choice when describing this dish.*

NEED:
- ½ lb of your favorite white fish (grouper, cod, sea bass, etc.)
- 2 small scoops of butter
- Pinch of dill weed and salt/pepper
- Splash of white wine (optional)
- 1 potato
- 2 handfuls of cheese (American or Cheddar)
- Small bunch of fresh broccoli

TO DO:
1) Place fish in a deep plate or shallow bowl and dab on butter, sprinkle dill weed and salt/pepper, and spoon on wine all over.
2) Cook fish for about 6 minutes (until it looks flaky).
3) Poke holes all around potato using a fork.
4) Wrap potato in paper towel and nuke for about 4 minutes (give or take).
5) Cut in half and add cheese and salt/pepper.
6) Cook broccoli in bowl half full of water for 3 minutes (or however soft/crunchy you like it).
7) Drain excess water.
8) Add cheese and allow to melt.

✓ Prep-time: 7 min
✓ Cook-time: about 15 min
✓ Cost Factor: $$
✓ Serves: 1

Grilled Chicken Caesar Salad

This dish offers crispy romaine lettuce and tender chicken (yes, you can nuke chicken).

NEED:
- 1 Caesar salad kit (I know, we are cheating!– but it's cost effective instead of buying a bottle of dressing, lettuce, parmesan cheese, and croutons)
- 1 chicken breast diced in cubes or buy packets of pre-cooked chicken

TO DO:
1) Use about half of Caesar salad kit (use whole if you're really hungry).
2) Mix a squirt of Caesar dressing (from the kit) and diced (bite-size) chicken in a bowl.
3) Nuke chicken for about 3 minutes on each side (Wash-up! Make sure chicken is cooked thoroughly).
4) Toss all together in a large bowl and kick back!

> ✓ Prep-time: 2 min
> ✓ Cook-time: 6 min
> ✓ Cost Factor: $
> ✓ Serves: 1

Breakfast Burrito

This is a fantastic way to eat a balanced breakfast in the dorm. Wrap it in a paper towel and munch as you walk to class.

NEED:
- 2 slices of bacon
- 1 soft tortilla
- 1 or 2 eggs
- Handful of shredded cheese
- ½ fresh tomato, diced
- Few dashes salt/pepper

TO DO:
1) Nuke bacon strips on a paper towel for about 3 minutes.
2) Cut into bite size chunks and sprinkle on tortilla.
3) Beat eggs in a glass cup or bowl and cook 1½ minutes for 2 eggs (should be good, but check to see if it needs more time).
4) Break apart eggs and place evenly on tortilla.
5) Sprinkle cheese.
6) Heat tortilla for about 15 seconds until cheese melts.
7) Top with diced tomatoes and salt/pepper.

✓ Prep-time: 4 min
✓ Cook-time: about 5 min
✓ Cost Factor: $
✓ Serves: 1

Spinach and Pancetta with Wild Rice

Vegetable, meat and grain will satisfy your hunger with a healthy combo of flavors. Now this is fine dining in your dorm!

NEED:

- ½ cup wild rice
- 2 large handfuls of spinach
- 3 strips of pancetta, bacon or sausage

TO DO:

1) Cook rice using microwaveable directions.
2) Place spinach in a bowl and nuke for about 1 minute or until cooked down.
3) Nuke pancetta for about 2 minutes on a paper towel (to collect grease).
4) Cut pancetta into bite size pieces.
5) Place rice in serving bowl, top with spinach and sprinkle pancetta on top.

> ✓ Prep-time: 3 min
> ✓ Cook-time: depends on rice cooking-time
> ✓ Cost Factor: $
> ✓ Serves: 1

Veggie *Love*

I have many college friends, who are 'confirmed' vegetarians. They frequently stress out over the lack of campus meal plans, snack options and basic cookbooks. Whether you're into 'vegetation', or not this chapter is for anyone who likes fun, fresh, colorful food! These recipes are considered to be repeat winners by my meatless friends.

Margarita Pizza

This is a classic and elegant pizza. This Italian dish tastes oh so FRESH! Big thick slices of tomato and fresh basil leaves will make your taste buds explode!

NEED:
- Few splashes olive oil
- 1 thin pizza crust
- 1 Roma tomato, thinly sliced
- ½ mozzarella ball in water, broken into chunks (can also use shredded mozzarella)
- 1 small handful of fresh basil, roughly torn
- Couple pinches salt/pepper

TO DO:
1) Preheat oven to 450°.
2) Drizzle a little olive oil on crust and spread with back of spoon.
3) Place tomato slices, mozzarella, and basil on top.
4) Season with salt and pepper and a light drizzle of olive oil.

- ✓ Prep-time: 6 min
- ✓ Cook-time: about 10 min
- ✓ Cost Factor: $
- ✓ Serves: 3

Asparagus and Cherry Tomato Angel Hair

A light and healthy dish that will satisfy all!

NEED:

- Dashes of olive oil
- 1 bunch asparagus, tough ends cut off, then cut in thirds
- 2 large handfuls of cherry tomatoes, sliced in half
- ½ box angel hair pasta (give whole wheat a whirl)
- 1 lemon
- Salt/Pepper
- Handful of grated parmesan cheese (if you don't have it, don't sweat it)

TO DO:

1) Preheat oven to 400°.
2) Drizzle olive oil over asparagus and tomatoes and bake for about 10 minutes on a baking sheet.
3) Boil/drain pasta according to box directions and place in large bowl.
4) Throw in roasted asparagus and cherry tomatoes.
5) Cut lemon in half and squeeze juices in bowl and add a few pinches of zest (grate only yellow part of lemon skin).
6) Drizzle in olive oil (about ¼ cup), add a few dashes of salt and pepper.
7) Toss together and sprinkle cheese on top. Enjoy!

- ✓ Prep-time: 8 min
- ✓ Cook-time: about 15 min
- ✓ Cost Factor: $
- ✓ Serves: 4

Roasted Veggie Couscous

Your recommended vegetable serving for the week will be completed with this dish. I have allowed for plenty of leftovers to munch on throughout the week. You're welcome!

NEED:

- 1 red pepper, cut into thin strips
- 2 large handfuls of baby carrots, sliced in half lengthwise
- ½ onion, thickly sliced
- 1 zucchini, quartered lengthwise, then cut into bite size chunks
- 2 handfuls mushrooms, cut in half
- Few splashes of olive oil
- Salt/Pepper
- 1 box of couscous (can do plain or a flavor - all up to you!)
- 2 handfuls of Parmesan cheese

TO DO:

1) Preheat oven to 450°.
2) Toss vegetables together on a baking sheet with olive oil and dashes of salt and pepper (I like to use my hands to make sure everything is coated) and roast for about 15 minutes until tender.
3) Cook cousous following box instructions (super simple!).
4) Toss cooked vegetables and couscous together in a large bowl.
5) Throw in the Parm! Mmm—mm!

- ✓ Prep-time: 12 min
- ✓ Cook-time: about 25 min
- ✓ Cost Factor: $
- ✓ Serves: 4

Eggplant Parmesan

This is another party in the mouth dish!! Tender, crispy eggplant coated in Italian seasoning, and served warm with melted cheese gives this dish an A+.

NEED:

- 2 large handfuls of flour
- 1 egg, beaten
- 2 large handfuls of Italian breadcrumbs
- 1 large eggplant sliced (about ½″)
- Few splashes of olive oil (eggplant soaks up olive oil fast, I recommend using grapeseed oil if on-hand)
- 2 large handfuls grated mozzarella or parmesan cheese
- ½ box pasta (any kind works; however, angel hair presents the best)
- 1 (25 oz) jar marinara sauce

> ✓ Prep-time: 8 min
> ✓ Cook-time: 25-35 min
> ✓ Cost Factor: $$
> ✓ Serves: 2-3

TO DO:

1) Preheat oven to 375°.
2) Put flour, egg, and breadcrumbs in separate bowls, take each slice of eggplant and throughly coat each piece in assembly-line.
3) Place eggplant and oil in a large pan on medium heat and allow it to get golden brown on each side (about 3 minutes per side).
4) Transfer eggplant onto baking sheet and bake for about 25 minutes until tender, about 2 minutes before you take it out, sprinkle mozzarella on each slice.
5) Boil/drain pasta according to box directions.
6) Heat marinara sauce on stove or in microwave.
7) Toss pasta and marinara sauce together and place eggplant on top.

Portobello and Swiss Sandwich

I hope everyone who reads this (even if you're not a vegetarian) gives this sandwich a shot! Imagine: biting into crispy bread then having your teeth strike through a juicy, meaty, shroom that was smothered in juices and topped with melted cheese. A real saliva rush !

NEED:

- Few splashes olive oil
- 2 large Portobello mushrooms, thinly sliced
- 1 small garlic clove, finely minced
- Splash Marsala or any white cooking wine
- ½ lemon, juice
- 4 slices of rustic bread (Ciabatta, Tuscan, or rolls)
- 2 slices of Swiss or any favorite cheese

✓ Prep-time: 5 min
✓ Cook-time: 10 min
✓ Cost Factor: $
✓ Serves: 2 (your roommate is going to want one)

TO DO:

1) Throw olive oil, mushrooms, and garlic in a pan.
2) Simmer on low heat for a few minutes (until soft), add Marsala and lemon juice.
3) Toast bread in toaster or in 400° oven for about 5 minutes or until crispy.
4) Assemble sandwich by taking two slices of bread and pouring the goodies from the pan (juices and all!) on top of bread.
5) Top with two slices of cheese. If Swiss doesn't melt enough put it in the microwave or oven until melted.
6) Top sandwich with the other piece of bread, cut in half, and mmmmm-mm!!!

Sinful Sweets

I love to bake, and these are my most requested desserts. They are all deliciously decadent, and piece of cake easy to make! No pun intended. There are variations of different types of desserts with commonly requested flavors to satisfy the sweet spot of the tongue. Bye-bye break-n-bake cookies and hello homemade goodies!

> " My culinary philosophy is simple: glorious food, good friends and great fun! "

Perfect Strawberry Cake

*Stop **facebook** stalking your ex and get in the kitchen and bake your new boyfriend a Valentine's cake! This is the perfect cake to make for any occasion! Fresh strawberries throughout the cake topped with homemade icing really makes this a special treat!*

NEED:

CAKE:

- 1 box of white cake mix
- 1 cup of vegetable oil
- 1 (3 oz) box of strawberry jell-o
- 4 eggs
- 1 cup of frozen strawberries, roughly chopped

ICING:

- 1 small box powdered sugar
- 1 stick of butter at room temp (may want to melt in microwave to avoid any chunks)
- 1 cup frozen strawberries, roughly chopped

> ✓ Prep-time: 20 min
> ✓ Bake-time: 25-20 min
> ✓ Cost Factor: $

TO DO:

1) Preheat oven to 350°.
2) Mix all cake ingredients together in large bowl and beat for about 3 minutes.
3) Pour into two greased round baking pans and bake.
4) Cool cake completely!!! (If you need to speed up the process, chill in freezer).
5) Now with the icing — beat all ingredients together (adding sugar slowly-it flies everywhere!) .
6) Spread on and between the two layers. Have fun with it!

Nana Lombardo's Secret Biscotti Recipe

This recipe came from a true Italian, my great-grandmother, and I get the same response every time I make it, "I usually don't like biscotti, but these are different." The smooth flavor paired with a burst of citrus is a superb dessert!

NEED:

- 4 eggs
- 1 ½ cup sugar
- 1 ¼ cup oil (vegetable or canola)
- 1 tbsp anise oil (found in grocery store next to vanilla extract)
- 1 tbsp vanilla extract
- 2 tbsp of orange juice
- ½ tbsp of orange zest (grate the orange peel)
- ¼ tbsp salt
- 3 tbsp baking powder
- 4 ½ cups flour (may need to add more for a thicker dough)

> ✓ Prep-time: 15 min
> ✓ Bake-time: about 40 min
> ✓ Cost Factor: $$

TO DO:

1) Preheat oven to 350°.
2) In a large bowl, beat eggs and sugar with electric mixer.
3) Add oil, a little at a time, then anise, vanilla, orange juice and zest.
4) Mix together salt, baking powder, flour and add to large bowl.
5) Shape into two large loaves (if not holding shape — put in refrigerator/freezer for 10 minutes).
6) Place loaves on cookie sheets and bake for 25 minutes.
7) Slice loaves into ½″ pieces and return to oven. Bake on each side until golden brown (about 5 minutes on each side).

Lemon-Berry Cupcakes

Tart-sweet berries with warm juices drizzled over moist, lemon cupcakes is a simple, light, and a stylish dessert that will have you wishing there were leftovers.

NEED:
- 1 box of lemon cake mix with the ingredients that are required (usually eggs, oil, and water)
- 1 small bag of frozen mixed berries (blueberries, strawberries, wild berries, etc…)
- 2 tablespoons of your favorite berry (strawberry, raspberry, blueberry, etc..) jam

TO DO:
1) Follow the lemon cake mix instructions. Let cupcakes cool.
2) Place berries and jam into a small pot or microwave cook until warm.
3) Serve with a drizzle of warm berries and juice over each cupcake.

- ✓ Prep-time: 10 min
- ✓ Bake-time: approximately 30 min
- ✓ Cost Factor: $

Blissful Banana Bread

This super easy and classic dish will get you drooling. Craving a snack between classes? Needing a slice with your morning coffee? Yearning a bite before bed? My banana will satisfy all the above.

NEED:

- 1 stick butter (at room temperature)
- 1 cup sugar
- 2 eggs
- 2 cups flour
- 1 teaspoon baking soda
- ½ teaspoon salt
- 4 ripe bananas mashed
- Nuts or chocolate chips optional

> ✓ Prep-time: 10 min
> ✓ Bake-time: 40-50 min
>   (check using a toothpick)
> ✓ Cost Factor: $

TO DO:

1) Preheat oven to 350°.
2) Beat butter and sugar together in a large bowl until creamy with electric mixer.
3) Beat in eggs.
4) Combine all dry ingredients, add to bowl.
5) Mash bananas, add to bowl.
6) Stir in nuts or chocolate chips if you like.
7) Pour into greased loaf pan and bake.

Almond Snowball Cookies

My all-time favorite cookie! My mom got this recipe from her roommate in her college days and has been making them ever since. These cookies are great for baking during the holidays, for parties, or for someone who needs comfort after bombing a final.

NEED:

- 2 ¼ cups flour
- ¾ cup sugar
- ¼ tsp baking powder
- ¼ tsp salt
- 1 cup shortening
- 1 egg
- 1 tsp almond flavoring
- 2 cups powdered sugar

> ✓ Prep-time: 10 min
> ✓ Bake-time: 10 min
> ✓ Cost Factor: $

TO DO:

1) Preheat oven to 375°.
2) Combine all dry ingredients in large bowl.
3) Add shortening to the dry ingredients, using two knives cross-slice until pea size crumbles form.
4) Add egg and almond, beat together.
5) Form round balls (a little smaller than a golf ball) and place on ungreased cookie sheets and bake.
6) Cool (completely!) then roll in powdered sugar.

Tropical Rum Cake

Is a friend turning 21? Stir up some excitement! Get your tush off the couch and in the kitchen! This is an excellent cake to bake to celebrate a 21st birthday!

NEED:

CAKE

- 1 pkg of yellow cake mix
- 1 (3.4 oz) pkg of instant pudding, vanilla OR coconut-cream flavor
- 4 eggs
- ½ cup cold water
- ½ cup oil
- ½ cup dark rum

ICING:

- 1 (8oz) can crushed pineapple with juice
- 1/3 cup dark rum
- 1 (3.4 oz) pkg of instant pudding, vanilla OR coconut-cream flavor
- 1 (9oz) tub whipped topping
- 1 cup flaked coconut

> ✓ Prep-time: 10 min
> ✓ Bake-time: 25-30 min (toothpick check- don't over bake!)
> ✓ Cost Factor: $$$

TO DO:

1) Preheat oven to 350°.
2) For the cake: beat all ingredients in large bowl.
3) Pour into greased round baking pans and bake.
4) For the icing — beat the pineapple, rum, and pudding together, fold in the whipped cream with a large spoon or spatula.
5) Cool cakes completely before slappin' the icing on and between layers.
6) Sprinkle the flaked coconut on top and between the layer.

Carefree Carrot Cake

It's the real deal! Moist, rich, and smooth flavors are the words of choice when describing this cake. Great to bake for the parents when they come to visit you.

NEED:

CAKE:

- 2 cups sugar
- 1½ cups canola oil
- 4 eggs
- 2 cups flour
- 2 tsp baking soda
- 4 tsp cinnamon
- 1 tsp salt
- ½ cup chopped nuts (optional)
- 3 cups freshly grated carrots

ICING:

- 2 cups confectioner's sugar
- ½ stick butter (at room temp)
- 8 oz container of cream cheese (at room temp)
- 2 tsp vanilla

> ✓ Prep-time: 25 min (carrots take some time to grate)
> ✓ Bake-time: 35-40 min (do the toothpick check)
> ✓ Cost Factor: $

TO DO:

1) Preheat oven to 350°.
2) Beat sugar, oil, and eggs together in large bowl.
3) Toss all dry ingredients together and add to large bowl.
4) Stir in nuts and carrots.
5) Pour into two greased round baking pans and bake.
6) For the icing — beat all ingredients together (add sugar slowly).
7) Cool cakes completely before spreading the icing on top and between layers.
8) Sprinkle extra grated carrots on top.

Gram's Cranberry Muffins

Shhh! This is a secret family recipe along with the biscotti. I'm confident enough to say this is the all-time best muffin. Thanks Gram! The buttermilk adds a tart, creamy flavor. If you aren't a fan of cranberries, you can substitute with blueberries. This is a moist, full flavored muffin, perfect during the fall season.

NEED:

- 1 cup chopped fresh cranberries
- 1 egg
- ¼ cup canola oil
- ¾ cup buttermilk
- 2 cups flour
- ½ tsp baking soda
- ½ tsp salt
- ¾ cup sugar
- Cinnamon and sugar

- ✓ Prep-time: 15 min
- ✓ Bake-time: 25 min
- ✓ Cost Factor: $

TO DO:

1) Preheat oven to 400°.
2) Chop cranberries in half.
3) Beat egg, oil, and buttermilk together in large bowl.
4) Mix all dry ingredients and add egg buttermilk mixture.
5) Stir in cranberries (don't over mix).
6) Spoon into greased (12 count) muffin pan.
7) Sprinkle top with cinnamon and sugar on top and bake.

Fruity-Tootie Crumble

So FAST, so EASY, so TASTY! This will take no time to throw together and gets your servings of healthy fruit in. Go ahead and indulge…

NEED:

CRUMBLE
- 1 ¼ cup flour
- 1 stick of butter
- ¼ cup sugar
- 1 tsp salt
- 1lb of sliced fruit (berries, apples, melons, oranges, whatever kind of fruit is on sale/in season)
- 3 tbsp of sugar

TO DO:

1) Preheat oven to 400°.
2) Mix flour, butter, sugar and salt together until course crumbles form.
3) Pour fruit into a shallow baking pan and sprinkle sugar on top.
4) Spread the crumbles evenly on top of the fruit and bake.

✓ Prep-time: 5 min
✓ Bake-time: 25-30 min
  (until golden brown)
✓ Cost Factor: $

Weekly *Planning*

While writing this cookbook, many college friends stated they would like to see a chapter on cooking meals that were exciting and nutritious enough to last for a week. That meant shopping once while pursuing the art of the leftover. Like many students, I felt overwhelmed until experimentation through trial and error paid off. If you follow my thinking process, you will feel confident when cruising the aisles for your week's supply of meals. This chapter will speed up store gathering skills, so you can have a great Sunday fun day!

October

1	2	3	4	5
8	9	10	11	12 Grille...
15	16	17 Tuna Pasta	18	19
22	23	24		26
29	30			

Need to know...

- I'm leaving most of the amounts of ingredients all up to you— don't go too crazy!
- All the meals listed are basic ideas so add your own little twist if desired.
- I recommend you bake/grill a couple chicken beasts on Sunday and store in refrigerator in order to save time.
- This is a BASIC chapter, I don't go into great detail, and I've kept it simple. I just want to give you quick and easy ideas/instructions to get you through the week.
- Eat leftovers and repeat the dishes!
- Save time and money, customize the leftovers to suit the occasion and appetite.
- Don't like chicken or bored of it? Substitute turkey, steak, ham, tofu, etc...or rotate them on different weeks to keep it exciting.

Sunday's Grocery List

- Bag of frozen or fresh chicken breasts
- 2 (6 oz) cans of tuna
- 1 box of pasta (penne, rigatoni)
- 1 bag of rice
- 1 carton of eggs
- 1 (15 oz) can of black beans
- 1 bunch of romaine lettuce
- 1 onion
- 2 tomatoes
- 1 (2 cup) bag of shredded cheese
- 1 loaf of bread
- 1 package soft tortilla shells
- 1 bag veggies (broccoli, carrots, snow peas)
- Oatmeal
- Fruit (pick your favorites)
- Basic condiments (hopefully you already have): olive oil, butter, your favorite salad dressing, maple syrup, salsa, soy-sauce, mayo, and salt and pepper.

BREAKFAST

- *Scrambled Eggs*
  - o Melt butter and soften diced onion in pan. Add scrambled eggs with cheese, top with diced tomato, salt/pepper, serve with a piece of toast.
- *Oatmeal with maple syrup*
  - o Microwave oatmeal, top with a small scoop of butter and a light drizzle of maple syrup.
- *French Toast*
  - o Soak two slices of bread on both sides in a bowl with a beaten egg, transfer onto a pan with melted butter, and cook both sides until golden-brown (about 2 minutes on each side). Top with a light drizzle of maple syrup or with fresh fruit and powdered sugar.
- *Breakfast Burrito*
  - o Scramble eggs with cheese and place on a warm tortilla shell with a scoop of salsa spread over the top. (See Dorm Dishes p. 84–91)

LUNCH

- *Tuna Salad*
  - o Place drained canned tuna in a bowl and stir in mayo, diced onion, salt/pepper, and handful of lettuce. Need more substance? Spread on a piece of toast or roll it in a tortilla wrap.
- *Chicken Quesadillas*
  - o Between two tortilla shells, place cut-up chicken breast, canned/drained black beans, shredded cheese, and salsa. Place in microwave to melt cheese.
- *Chicken Ranch Wrap*
  - o In a tortilla, place sliced grilled chicken, cheese, lettuce and Ranch. (See Study Time Snacks p. 12–21).
- *Broccoli Chicken Pasta*
  - o Steam broccoli until soft and melt cheese on top. Mix into cooked pasta and chunks of grilled chicken. Top with either olive oil and salt/pepper or your favorite salad dressing.

- *Chicken Stir-Fry and Rice*
  - While rice is cooking, cook diced chicken with soy sauce and add sliced broccoli, carrots, and snow peas. Mix together and serve on rice.
- *Roasted Vegetable Pasta*
  - Roast chopped vegetables in oven with olive oil and salt/pepper until tender. Stir in pasta with shredded cheese and olive oil.
- *Chicken, Beans, and Rice*
  - Combine cooked, warm rice and beans and top with marinated chicken, fresh-diced tomatoes, and a sprinkle of cheese.
- *Tuna Pasta*
  - Drain canned tuna and mix in mayo, onion, salt/pepper and pasta. (See Pinchin' Pennies p. 64–72)

Special Thanks!

These are the people who were around daily helping me get the show on the road... :)

- David Dismukes- Your extraordinary photography skills, creative ideas, and many helpful connections allowed me to get this cookbook off to a wonderful start!

- Toby and Char Warren- The advice you both have given me will forever hold close to my heart. I'm so grateful to have met such a stimulating, inspirational, and loving power couple!

- Dave Kempf and FRP staff- With all your efforts, you helped me bring this book to the finish line.

There were many people who inspired me to write this cookbook and I can't thank you all enough!

- My sister, Jenni- Your constant encouragement and love! You showed me the importance of simplicity when cooking! Also responsible for my very first le creuset bowl!

- Mom- World's best role model!- and not just in the kitchen!- I secretly (well, not a secret anymore) want to be just like you! Your healthy cooking was a great example growing up and the amount of time you whip a dish together is unreal!

- Dad- Always demonstrating the importance of imagination and creativity. We have thrown together some interesting and delicious sandwiches over the years!

- Gram- Original and inventive – no one will ever beat your cranberry muffins!

- Grandma Shea- Never play with your hair in the kitchen!- I'll never forget that! Your authentic Italian cooking was such an inspiration!

- Grandpa Shea- O'Shea's Restaurant alone is enough said! Oh yeah, and your famous clam chowder!

- Nanny Lombardo- Another superb Italian chef who is responsible for the biscottis!

- Grandpa Hoffman- Always showing the business side of every endeavor.

- Heather- Everyday positive attitude and loving food as much as I do!

- Brit and Emily- Making me aware that some people really have no idea where to begin in the kitchen... love you guys!

- Sarah- Continual support since 5th grade and always down to chow down with me!

- My pup, Ellie Sue- Never turning down a bite of my experimental cooking!

- Boring Professors- Thought of my most tasty dishes in these classes- thanks!

- My love for cooking started at my kindergarten cooking theme birthday party!

Index

Appetizers. *See* Dips; Granola; Salsas; Snacks

Apple
Cottage Cheese, Fruit and Granola, 18
Jazzed-up Rice Cake, 19
Marshmallow and Lime Fresh Fruit Salad, 36
Spinach Apple Salad, 57
Yogurt Burst, 63

Asparagus
Asparagus and Cherry Tomato Angel Hair, 95
Grilled Shrimp and Asparagus, 60

Avocado
Guacamole Dip, 25
Mexican Dip, 29

Bacon
Breakfast Burrito, 90
Cucumber and Bacon Sandwich, 35
Fancy Mac and Cheese, 50
Healthy Eggy Goodness, 62
Spinach and Pancetta with Wild Rice, 91

Banana
Blissful Banana Bread, 105
Frozen Banana Popsicles, 16
Strawberry-Banana Smoothie, 55
Terrific Trail Mix, 15
Yogurt Burst, 63

Beans
BBQ Chicken Legs and Baked Beans, 68
Chicken, Beans, and Rice, 115
Chicken Quesadillas, 114
Healthy and Hearty Dip, 27
Homemade Chili, 72
Hotdog and Baked Beans, 86
Mexican Dip, 29
Mexican Salad, 37
New Orleans Rib Sticker, 66

Beef. *See* also Veal
Homemade Chili, 72
Pasta Meat Salad, 71
Steak Stir-Fry, 83
Super Bowl Dip, 31

Berries
Lemon-Berry Cupcakes, 104
Vanilla-Berry Smoothie, 17

Beverages
Strawberry-Banana Smoothie, 55
Vanilla-Berry Smoothie, 17

Breads. *See* French Toast
Blissful Banana Bread, 105
Gram's Cranberry Muffins, 109

Broccoli
Broccoli Chicken Pasta, 114
Chicken Stir-Fry and Rice, 115
Italian Pasta Salad, 34
Steak Stir-Fry, 83
White Fish with Cheesy Broccoli and a Baked Potato, 88

Cakes
Carefree Carrot Cake, 108
Lemon-Berry Cupcakes, 104
Perfect Strawberry Cake, 102
Tropical Rum Cake, 107

Carrots
Carefree Carrot Cake, 108
Chicken Stir-Fry and Rice, 115
Italian Pasta Salad, 34
Roasted Veggie Couscous, 96
Steak Stir-Fry, 83
Veggie Soup, 54

Chicken
BBQ Chicken Legs and Baked Beans, 68
BBQ Chicken Pizza, 80
Broccoli Chicken Pasta, 114
Buffalo Chicken Dip, 28
Chicken, Beans, and Rice, 115
Chicken Quesadillas, 114
Chicken Ranch Wrap, 20, 114
Chicken Spaghetti, 70
Chicken Stir-Fry and Rice, 115
Grilled Chicken Caesar Salad, 89
Ground Chicken Meatballs, 21
Homemade Chili, 72
Mexican Salad, 37
Pasta Meat Salad, 71
Rosemary Orange Roasted Chicken, 78
Viva La Difference Lasagna, 44

Chocolate
Frozen Banana Popsicles, 16
Terrific Trail Mix, 15

Clams
O'Shea's Famous Clam Chowder, 49

Cookies
Almond Snowball Cookies, 106
Nana Lombardo's Secret Biscotti Recipe, 103

Corn
Erin's Ramen P-a-a-r-r-t-a-y, 69
Healthy and Hearty Dip, 27
Mexican Salad, 37

Cost Factor $
Almond Snowball Cookies, 106
Asparagus and Cherry Tomato Angel Hair, 95
BBQ Chicken Legs and Baked Beans, 68
BBQ Chicken Pizza, 80
Beer Brats and Caramelized Onions, 39
Blissful Banana Bread, 105
Breakfast Burrito, 90
Buffalo Chicken Dip, 28
Carefree Carrot Cake, 108
Chicken Ranch Wrap, 20
Chicken Spaghetti, 70
Classy Grilled Cheese, 47
Cream Cheese and Salsa Dip, 30
Creamy Dreamy Mashies, 48
Erin's Ramen P-a-a-r-r-t-a-y, 69
Fancy Mac and Cheese, 50
Frozen Banana Popsicles, 16
Fruity-Tootie Crumble, 110
Gram's Cranberry Muffins, 109
Grilled Chicken Caesar Salad, 89
Grilled Turkey Burgers, 59
Ground Turkey Meatloaf, 77
Guacamole Dip, 25
Healthy and Hearty Dip, 27
Healthy Eggy Goodness, 62
Homemade Chili, 72
Hotdog and Baked Beans, 86
Hummus Dip, 24
Italian Pasta Salad, 34
Jazzed-up Rice Cake, 19
Lemon-Berry Cupcakes, 104
Margarita Pizza, 94
Marshmallow and Lime Fresh Fruit Salad, 36
New Orleans Rib Sticker, 66
Orange Cup Sweet Potatoes, 40
Pasta Meat Salad, 71
Peanut Butter and Jelly French Toast, 47
Pear and Gorgonzola Salad, 56
Perfect Strawberry Cake, 102
Portobello and Swiss Sandwich, 98
Quesadilla, 86
Ramen Tuna, 69
Roasted Veggie Couscous, 96
Rosemary Orange Roasted Chicken, 78
Shrimp and Grits, 87
Spaghetti Squash, 61
Spinach and Pancetta with Wild Rice, 91
Spinach Apple Salad, 57
Spinach Artichoke Dip, 26
Strawberry-Banana Smoothie, 55
Strawberry Feta Salad, 58
Super Bowl Dip, 31
Sweet Potato Fries, 14
Tuna Melt, 46
Tuna Pasta, 67

Vanilla-Berry Smoothie, 17
Veggie Soup, 54
Yogurt Burst, 63

Cost Factor $$
Any White Fish Dish, The, 61
Cottage Cheese, Fruit and
   Granola, 18
Cucumber and Bacon
   Sandwich, 35
Eggplant Parmesan, 97
Grilled Shrimp and
   Asparagus, 60
Ground Chicken Meatballs, 21
Mexican Dip, 29
Mexican Salad, 37
Nana Lombardo's Secret
   Biscotti Recipe, 103
O'Shea's Famous Clam
   Chowder, 49
Pork Chops Smothered in
   Caramelized Onions, 81
Red Pepper and Dill Salmon, 79
Shrimp Scampi, 76
"Simple Salad," The, 38
Steak Stir-Fry, 83
Viva La Difference Lasagna, 44
White Fish with Cheesy
   Broccoli and a Baked
   Potato, 88

Cost Factor $$$
Terrific Trail Mix, 15
Tropical Rum Cake, 107
Veal Scaloppini, 82

Cottage Cheese
Cottage Cheese, Fruit and
   Granola, 18

Cucumbers
Cucumber and Bacon
   Sandwich, 35
"Simple Salad," The, 38

Dips
Buffalo Chicken Dip, 28
Cream Cheese and Salsa
   Dip, 30
Guacamole Dip, 25
Healthy and Hearty Dip, 27
Hummus Dip, 24
Mexican Dip, 29
Spinach Artichoke Dip, 26
Super Bowl Dip, 31

Egg Dishes
Breakfast Burrito, 90, 114
French Toast, 114
Healthy Eggy Goodness, 62
Scrambled Eggs, 114

Fish. *See also* Tuna
Any White Fish Dish, The, 61
Red Pepper and Dill Salmon, 79

White Fish with Cheesy
   Broccoli and a Baked
   Potato, 88

French Toast
Peanut Butter and Jelly French
   Toast, 47

Fruit. *See also* Apple; Avocado;
   Banana; Berries; Grape;
   Orange; Pineapple;
   Strawberry
Cottage Cheese, Fruit and
   Granola, 18
Fruity-Tootie Crumble, 110
Pear and Gorgonzola Salad, 56

Granola
Cottage Cheese, Fruit and
   Granola, 18
Terrific Trail Mix, 15
Yogurt Burst, 63

Grape
Marshmallow and Lime Fresh
   Fruit Salad, 36

Ham
Classy Grilled Cheese, 47
Quesadilla, 86

Mushrooms
Portobello and Swiss
   Sandwich, 98
Shrimp Scampi, 76
Veggie Soup, 54

Nuts. *See also* Peanuts
Strawberry Feta Salad, 58

Onions
Beer Brats and Caramelized
   Onions, 39
Pork Chops Smothered in
   Caramelized Onions, 81

Orange
Orange Cup Sweet Potatoes, 40
Rosemary Orange Roasted
   Chicken, 78
Yogurt Burst, 63

Pasta
Asparagus and Cherry Tomato
   Angel Hair, 95
Broccoli Chicken Pasta, 114
Chicken Spaghetti, 70
Eggplant Parmesan, 97
Fancy Mac and Cheese, 50
Ground Chicken Meatballs, 21
Italian Pasta Salad, 34
Mexican Salad, 37
Pasta Meat Salad, 71
Roasted Vegetable Pasta, 115
Shrimp Scampi, 76

Tuna Pasta, 67, 115
Viva La Difference Lasagna, 44

Peanut Butter
Jazzed-up Rice Cake, 19
Peanut Butter and Jelly French
   Toast, 47

Peanuts
Terrific Trail Mix, 15

Pineapple
Marshmallow and Lime Fresh
   Fruit Salad, 36
Tropical Rum Cake, 107

Pizza
BBQ Chicken Pizza, 80
Margarita Pizza, 94

Pork. *See also* Bacon; Ham;
   Sausage
Pork Chops Smothered in
   Caramelized Onions, 81

Potatoes
Creamy Dreamy Mashies, 48
O'Shea's Famous Clam
   Chowder, 49
White Fish with Cheesy
   Broccoli and a Baked
   Potato, 88

Poultry. *See* Chicken; Turkey

Quesadillas
Chicken Quesadillas, 114
Quesadilla, 86

Ramen Noodles
Erin's Ramen P-a-a-r-r-t-a-y, 69
Ramen Tuna, 69

Rice
Chicken, Beans, and Rice, 115
Chicken Stir-Fry and Rice, 115
New Orleans Rib Sticker, 66
Spinach and Pancetta with
   Wild Rice, 91

Salads
Grilled Chicken Caesar Salad, 89
Italian Pasta Salad, 34
Marshmallow and Lime Fresh
   Fruit Salad, 36
Mexican Salad, 37
Pear and Gorgonzola Salad, 56
"Simple Salad," The, 38
Spinach Apple Salad, 57
Strawberry Feta Salad, 58
Tuna Pasta, 67
Tuna Salad, 114

Salsas
Chicken Quesadillas, 114

Index

Cream Cheese and Salsa
  Dip, 30
Mexican Dip, 29
Quesadilla, 86

Sandwiches
  Beer Brats and Caramelized
    Onions, 39
  Chicken Ranch Wrap, 20
  Classy Grilled Cheese, 47
  Cucumber and Bacon
    Sandwich, 35
  Hotdog and Baked Beans, 86
  Peanut Butter and Jelly French
    Toast, 47
  Portobello and Swiss
    Sandwich, 98
  Tuna Melt, 46

Sausage
  Beer Brats and Caramelized
    Onions, 39
  Hotdog and Baked Beans, 86
  New Orleans Rib Sticker, 66
  Spinach and Pancetta with
    Wild Rice, 91

Seafood
  Any White Fish Dish, The, 61
  Erin's Ramen P-a-a-r-r-t-a-y, 69
  Grilled Shrimp and
    Asparagus, 60
  O'Shea's Famous Clam
    Chowder, 49
  Pasta Meat Salad, 71
  Ramen Tuna, 69
  Red Pepper and Dill Salmon, 79
  Shrimp and Grits, 87
  Shrimp Scampi, 76
  Tuna Melt, 46
  Tuna Pasta, 67
  White Fish with Cheesy
    Broccoli and a Baked
    Potato, 88

Shrimp
  Grilled Shrimp and
    Asparagus, 60
  Shrimp and Grits, 87
  Shrimp Scampi, 76

Smoothies
  Strawberry-Banana
    Smoothie, 55
  Vanilla-Berry Smoothie, 17

Snacks
  Buffalo Chicken Dip, 28
  Cream Cheese and Salsa
    Dip, 30

Guacamole Dip, 25
Hummus Dip, 24
Jazzed-up Rice Cake, 19
Mexican Dip, 29
Spinach Artichoke Dip, 26
Super Bowl Dip, 31
Sweet Potato Fries, 14
Terrific Trail Mix, 15
Yogurt Burst, 63

Snow Peas
  Chicken Stir-Fry and Rice, 115
  Steak Stir-Fry, 83

Soups
  O'Shea's Famous Clam
    Chowder, 49
  Veggie Soup, 54

Spinach
  Healthy Eggy Goodness, 62
  Pear and Gorgonzola Salad, 56
  Spinach and Pancetta with
    Wild Rice, 91
  Spinach Apple Salad, 57
  Spinach Artichoke Dip, 26
  Strawberry Feta Salad, 58

Squash
  Spaghetti Squash, 61

Strawberry
  Marshmallow and Lime Fresh
    Fruit Salad, 36
  Perfect Strawberry Cake, 102
  Strawberry-Banana
    Smoothie, 55
  Strawberry Feta Salad, 58
  Yogurt Burst, 63

Sweet Potatoes
  Orange Cup Sweet Potatoes, 40
  Sweet Potato Fries, 14

Sweets
  Almond Snowball Cookies, 106
  Blissful Banana Bread, 105
  Carefree Carrot Cake, 108
  Frozen Banana Popsicles, 16
  Fruity-Tootie Crumble, 110
  Gram's Cranberry Muffins, 109
  Lemon-Berry Cupcakes, 104
  Nana Lombardo's Secret
    Biscotti Recipe, 103
  Perfect Strawberry Cake, 102
  Tropical Rum Cake, 107

Tomatoes
  Asparagus and Cherry Tomato
    Angel Hair, 95

Guacamole Dip, 25
Healthy and Hearty Dip, 27
Margarita Pizza, 94
Mexican Salad, 37
"Simple Salad," The, 38
Super Bowl Dip, 31

Tortillas
  Breakfast Burrito, 90, 114
  Chicken Quesadillas, 114
  Chicken Ranch Wrap, 20, 114
  Quesadilla, 86

Tuna
  Erin's Ramen P-a-a-r-r-t-a-y, 69
  Ramen Tuna, 69
  Tuna Melt, 46
  Tuna Pasta, 67, 115
  Tuna Salad, 114

Turkey
  Grilled Turkey Burgers, 59
  Ground Turkey Meatloaf, 77
  Homemade Chili, 72
  Pasta Meat Salad, 71
  Quesadilla, 86

Veal
  Veal Scaloppini, 82

Vegetables. See also Asparagus;
    Beans; Broccoli; Carrots;
    Corn; Cucumbers;
    Mushrooms; Onions;
    Potatoes; Snow Peas;
    Spinach; Squash; Sweet
    Potatoes; Tomatoes;
    Zucchini
  Creamy Dreamy Mashies, 48
  Eggplant Parmesan, 97
  Margarita Pizza, 94
  Portobello and Swiss
    Sandwich, 98
  Roasted Vegetable Pasta, 115
  Roasted Veggie Couscous, 96
  "Simple Salad," The, 38
  Spaghetti Squash, 61
  Veggie Soup, 54

Yogurt
  Vanilla-Berry Smoothie, 17
  Yogurt Burst, 63

Zucchini
  Roasted Veggie Couscous, 96

1. Study Time Snacks

2. Decadent Dips

3. Crowd Pleasers

4. Comfort Foods

5. Dropping the Freshman 15

6. Pinchin' Pennies

7. Date Night Dinners

8. Dorm Dishes

9. Veggie Love

10. Sinful Sweets

11. Weekly Planning

I can't wait to share my affordable, healthy, simple and quick dishes that will change the way you think about college cuisine!

-Julie

www.collegecookingwithjulie.com
collegecookingwithjulie@gmail.com